A LIFE TRANSFORMED - BY ACCIDENT

AN INSPIRATIONAL MEMOIR

HELEN DECKER LIERE

Outskirts Press, Inc.
Denver, Colorado

To Ray, Aaron, and Karyn:
You truly light up my life

Table of Contents

Acknowledgements...ix

Introduction..xi

Chapter 1   The Day..1

Chapter 2   The Hospital...11

Chapter 3   Marooned in the Family Room.................25

Chapter 4   Meet the Family Caregivers.......................43

Chapter 5   Rehabilitation...57

Chapter 6   Trying To Work Things Out.......................75

Chapter 7   New Directions..93

Chapter 8   Knowing and Doing What Matters:
Faith...109

Chapter 9   Knowing and Doing What Matters:
Family and Friends...................................127

Chapter 10   Knowing and Doing What Matters:
Health (Physical and Mental)...................141

Chapter 11   Knowing and Doing What Matters:
Helping Others...161

Chapter 12   Decide to Change.....................................181

Chapter 13   Study Guide..185

Acknowledgements

I want to thank my family and all my friends, who I feel were true angels doing God's work by providing selfless love and support during my recovery. Most of you are identified in the book as I tell my story. Included among my family and friends are my Methodist church families, Pastor Gene, and Pastor Pam. I hope you will all be able to feel how much your help and presence meant and means to me. I thank you from the bottom of my heart.

Of course, a special and eternal place in my heart is held for my husband Ray, my son Aaron, and my daughter Karyn. I do not even want to contemplate where or who I would be without you. You have sustained me, encouraged me, loved me, and made my life full of joy and hope. The words "thank you" hardly seem enough.

I want to acknowledge the heroic efforts of the paramedics, the Life Flight staff, and all of my doctors. My main orthopedic doctor, Doctor Woll, will always have a special place in my heart. Dr. Woll, you are a man of few words but, lucky for me, you are a man of great skill and caring.

While I had many difficulties with the legal system, I would also like to thank Megan Glor, the lawyer who handled my disability insurance policy claim with such knowledge and grace. You are a special lawyer who helps people when they are feeling hurt and powerless.

And where would this book have been without my editor, Vinnie Kinsella, of Declaration Editing! While it sometimes took me a while to accept your advice, I have no doubt that this book is so much better because of that advice. You truly helped me focus, and you did that with kindness and expertise.

Introduction

This is the story of my personal transformation after a near fatal auto crash on February 3, 1994. I was 47 years old and a proud mother of two college students and the proud wife of another college student (my husband was working on his PhD). I was a hard-working and successful business owner who made the most of every minute. Ironically, I was also a traffic safety educator. My life changed abruptly that day, although the changes were just beginning and some of them took years for me to accept.

Since it has been several years since this life-changing event in my life, it is worth asking why I am writing about it after all this time. In fact, I have talked very little about my experiences and feelings related to my car crash and the changes in my life since the crash. I have no idea whether this is at all typical of people who have come close to death. The thing is, I never felt like I was going to die, so why I didn't feel more like talking about my experiences until now, I do not know. It is probably more related to who I am and how I was raised. When I was growing up, my family did not talk about personal things or feelings. You kept those to yourself. And my story is definitely personal and emotional.

It has also taken me several years to recognize just how much I have gained as well as how much I have lost as a result of my near fatal auto crash. I fought my loss by denying it. I tried to do the things I had always done. And when I ran into stone walls, I just did not think about it. I told everyone I was doing just fine, and I tried very hard to believe it.

So why write about all of this now? In a nutshell, I hope that others, especially those who have lost some physical ability, will benefit from reading about my experiences and what I have learned from them. After all, there are over two million people injured in traffic crashes each year. And even if you are fortunate enough to avoid such a dramatic life-changing event as mine, you may encounter many of the changes I have had to deal with as you age or face a serious illness. I will be richly rewarded if in writing about my experiences, someone is better prepared for his or her personal tragic challenge.

I also think I now know the reinvented me. I have finally worked through my changes, and writing this book helped me complete the process and provided a means of talking about it. I find that I agree with Arthur Schlesinger (*A Life in the Twentieth Century*), that the great benefit of writing is self-discovery, although "no one can probably ever truly know oneself – or anyone else".

Now one may wonder just how good my memory is after all of these years. And I will admit that I sometimes do leave one room and forget just what it was I was going to do. However, thanks to my husband, Ray, I did write some of my thoughts and activities in a journal for part of my recovery time. I would also agree nonetheless with Tennessee Williams' observation that "memory is seated predominantly in the heart."

I need to explain my use of the word *crash* throughout my story when most people might think I should use the word *accident*. It is a very conscious choice of words. Among traffic safety advocates, the word *crash* is used because most crashes are not accidents. They are very preventable and explained by bad choices, such as driving too fast or drinking. Such is the case in my crash. Then, one might ask why I use the word *accident* in the book title. Most importantly, I do not think my crash was planned by God and neither was my transformation. In that sense my transformation was an *accident* – an unforeseen or un-planned event. And I was playing off the common use of the word *accident*.

We all face challenges in life, and in particular life-chang-ing events. How we respond to them tells us a lot about ourselves and our fellow womankind and mankind. As each of us learns more about the human experience and the meaning of life, it seems important that we share our thoughts in the hope that we may increase our understanding of the importance of life and the responsibilities we have to each other.

My aim is that those of you who have suffered a tragedy or life-changing event will find hope and encouragement through hearing about my experience and what I have found helpful in dealing with loss. You may just find that you are able to say, "I felt like that too. It's good to know that I am not alone in feeling that way." Or you may be encouraged or empowered by my discussion on what helped me or what I learned, as I reinvented myself and found my new direction.

I think you will find my story both meaningful and interesting. You will learn just how this successful independent woman, who was raised to believe that with hard work you could accomplish your dreams, ended up in the wrong place at the wrong time. My major life experiences are woven into my story of recovery with humor. My story is one that involves a tragic crash, major health problems, a loving family and friends, losing a business, regaining health, and redirecting a life. And along the way there were lots of tears, laughter, love, and faith. It is a transformation story more than a survival story. It is a story I now feel compelled to tell.

1

The Day

"... Into each life some rain must fall ..."

Henry Wadsworth Longfellow
"The Rainy Day"

How many times have you heard, "You never know what tomorrow will bring?" I always thought it was a somewhat meaningless statement. Of course, we do not know what tomorrow will bring, but being a very optimistic person, I always thought it could only be something good, maybe even exciting. Well, I am writing to tell you the statement has a lot more to say than I thought. It now seems only too clear to me that each day is very precious and our time on this planet is tenuous. You see, I experienced a life-changing day that started out like many other tomorrows, and I had no idea how different things – and I – would be after that day.

The day, February 3, 1994 to be exact, started early. I had lots to do. At 47 years old, I was your typical workaholic consultant who put in at least 10-12 hours each day. It was easy. I enjoyed my work. I helped nonprofit and govern-mental organizations do their special work better, or I did work they could not do or did not want to do. For example, I operated a child safety seat resource center that educated people on the correct use of child safety seats, wrote grants for mental health programs to help drug-addicted mothers and their children, facilitated planning sessions for boards of directors of domestic violence shelters and libraries, advised on contracting for public services, and facilitated continuous improvement standards for aging services. It was a career with variety and challenge, and I felt like I was also helping people who needed help.

I also found it easy and necessary to work those long hours because my husband Ray had gone back to college to get his PhD, one of his life goals that he was now getting the chance to fulfill. Ray has been a very special partner for two-thirds of my life, and we have always supported each other's goals. For example, he had supported me when I went back to Portland State University to get my Masters in Public Administration. Our children were very young and he took care of them after long days at work while I was at school.

I was more than willing to support his academic pursuit, as I knew how much it meant to him. The decision for him to go back to school did create some extra stress for me as the main breadwinner because our two children, Aaron and Karyn, were also in college. Obviously, we became very versed in student loans. In fact, Ray and Aaron were both at Oregon State University, and Aaron's fraternity brothers were quite amazed that his dad would join them for cards and beer once in a while (I was assured that it was only once in a while).

At this time, Ray was living on campus at Oregon State University and came home each weekend. We both made sure that our weekends were work-free, and those weekends were a lot of fun. Of course, we had to watch our money, but we always had a lot to tell each other and we always ate well. After all, I did not have to cook much during the week, so it was actually fun to fix something special for Ray when he was home. And Ray also shared in wearing the chef's hat, as he is very good at barbequing. Often we would just stay home with a fire in the fireplace, rent a movie, and enjoy a bottle of wine. In short, we agreed the short-term sacrifice was worth the goal and we tried to make it as enjoyable (or maybe as painless) as possible.

I had spent the night before my life-changing day in Madras, Oregon, which is located just on the eastern side of the Cascade Mountains in central Oregon, about 2 ½ hours east of my office in Oregon City. Madras is a small rural community (about 5,000 population in 1994) where agriculture is the main industry. I loved going to Oregon's small towns, meeting with the local citizens, learning about their communities, and helping them with their traffic safety issues. In Madras, I was doing work as part of my contract with the Oregon Department of Transportation to develop the Child Safety Seat Resource Center, another very worthwhile and needed project. The nonuse and incorrect use of child safety seats was, and still is, a major cause of deaths and injuries to children under four years of age. I had started the Child Safety Seat Resource Center to provide information and assistance on the correct use of child safety seats.

On the night of February 2, I was conducting a workshop at the request of the Madras Police Department. The workshop was held at the Madras Senior Center and attended by about twelve individuals consisting of police and fire officials and other citizens. These workshops were always very interactive, as those attending were motivated students. They cared about their community and its youngest residents. Once they understood how to install traffic safety seats correctly, they would hold drive-in check-up clinics where they would help mothers and fathers with their children's seats. When I left the Senior Center, I also can remember noting how clear the night was, the stars and moon so bright in the clean cold high desert air.

I was asked to have breakfast with the city police officers on the morning of February 3, but declined since I wanted to get that early start back to my office. It was foggy and chilly when I started back about 7:30 a.m. Fog in this part of Oregon can be very dense, and I was concerned about frost or ice as I started up Highway 26 towards Government Camp on Mt. Hood in my Nissan Altima. I was relieved when I passed the summit of the pass (approximately 4500 feet) about two hours later and the sun came out.

I was soon in very familiar territory as I headed further down the west side of the mountain past Welches. I had lived my first 18 years on a farm my grandfather homesteaded in Boring, Oregon. (At least Boring was the postal delivery district I lived in. I have endured many a joke growing up about whether Boring was boring, but just for the record, Boring was named after an early resident of the area, W. H. Boring. Let's just say that Boring was "laid back.") I attended Sandy Grade School and Sandy High School since I lived in the Sandy School District. Some of my high school friends lived "up the mountain" in the area I was driving through. I marveled again at the natural beauty of the Mt. Hood National Forest: the large Douglas fir trees, the wild rhododendrons, the trails for hiking, or, at this time of year, for snow shoeing or cross-country skiing.

As the Righteous Brothers sang their soulful songs of the sixties on my car's tape deck, I thought about those teenage years when I was so driven to succeed. I wanted straight A's and to be student body president, and it had all happened for me. I guess that speaks to the importance of vision and determination, not to mention optimism. I was a very lucky kid to have grown up in this area and in an environment where I was encouraged to be self-reliant, independent, and hardworking. That was the way to reach your goals and be all you could be. And I was a dreamer who set goals for each stage of my life. I wanted to be somebody who made a difference.

I stayed in the right lane of the two west-bound lanes as it was in sun, whereas the left lane was still in shade and I could not tell whether there was frost or not. The only separation between the east- and west-bound lanes was double yellow centerlines. I also kept my speed at about 50 mph in the 55 mph zone even though people were passing me. Although the road looked okay, I just felt a little uneasy. I have never liked to drive in frosty or snowy conditions. Usually, I cancelled meetings if bad weather was predicted on my routes to community meetings.

All of a sudden, I noticed a blue pickup truck careening around a corner in the oncoming lanes and swerving out of control. I started to reach for the brake with my foot, wondering if it would hit the vehicle in front of me (a small station wagon). I started to turn toward the shoulder, just in case, when everything stopped in time. I am not sure how she (the driver of the pickup was a young woman) hit me head on instead of the vehicle in front of me, but the next thing I knew I was sort of awake and sort of in a dream. It was like I was observing something I was not a part of. Initially, I heard no sounds – not even the sirens of the emergency vehicles. They just appeared. I smelled nothing. I felt nothing.

Time just seemed to stop and so did my thought process, I guess, as I did not try to figure out if I was hurt. I just sat there. I did not try to move, although I do not remember thinking I was hurt.

A very nice man (I later learned from the county sheriff that he was a truck driver who had been driving behind me) came up and knelt down by my window and talked to me. He asked me how I was and I said I thought I was okay, but again I did not try to move. He said he thought the air bag must have saved my life. I felt too tired to talk with him, but remember thinking that his observation was rather a strong statement. Sure, I was alive, but then why shouldn't I be? I just did not take in exactly what had happened. I had no idea how badly I was hurt as I had no pain right then. It is rather amazing how the human nervous system protects you from pain. I guess that is called being in shock.

However, a problem soon developed. A fireman (he had the distinguishing yellow coat on) came over and asked me if I could breathe, and I said I was having a little trouble getting air. It then got worse and I was having a lot of trouble getting air. It was a very panicky desperate feeling, and I expressed that loud and clear. Fortunately, the fireman had oxygen for me and I could relax again somewhat in my dreamlike state.

Then the firemen wanted to get me out of the car. I went to move but could not. I was surprised I could not just open the door and get out, but my body seemed frozen. They apologized but said they were going to have to lift me out. I was not sure why they were apologizing, and then somehow my nervous system let me down − I screamed. There was unbelievable pain, mainly in my right hip and leg, but short-lived as I blacked out as they got me to the road. I then lost track of time for a little while.

I now know why they say you should always be wearing clean underwear. Well, at least one of the reasons. When I came to again on the pavement, they were cutting away all my clothing. I will admit I really did not care; in fact, I only remember little pieces here and there. I do remember being cold. I am not sure what all they did to get me ready for transport, but I was transported by ambulance for a short distance until the Life Flight helicopter met us at some agreed upon landing spot.

The Life Flight helicopter had taken the driver of the pickup to one of the two trauma hospitals in Portland first. They were then to return for me and take me to the other trauma hospital, Oregon Health Sciences University. Somehow the ambulance driver had communicated with the helicopter pilot about where to meet.

Every so often when I was in the ambulance and then the helicopter, I would hear the emergency service people talking. The people in the ambulance were upset that the helicopter was not getting there as fast as they wanted. Then the people in the helicopter kept trying to keep me awake. I remember being somewhat irritated about their constant questioning. I remember them mispronouncing my last name over and over and my having to correct them when I could. (By the way, Liere is pronounced like Leary.) I imagine their purpose was to try and keep me conscious. But I was so tired.

The most outstanding memory of the Life Flight was the horrible smell of diesel and the very loud sound of the engine and propellers. I also seemed to be in a tunnel or at least a very confined space. The next lucent (relatively speaking) memory was the emergency room where once again people were apologizing to me. This time they were doctors. You can always recognize a doctor no matter how fuzzy your mind is otherwise. The doctors were sorry that they did not have time to wait for anesthesia to take effect and help with the pain before inserting chest tubes. They quietly explained that I had two collapsed lungs and they needed to drill into my chest immediately. I said, "Go ahead and do what you have to." Like I had a choice. Like I even knew what that meant. When the drill started to grind something that was part of me, I screamed and lost consciousness.

I woke up in intensive care with lots of machines around me and tubes coming out of me. The ceiling was grey and the whole room seemed large, grey, and cold. I saw a nurse over by some machines. My husband, Ray, and children, Aaron and Karyn, came in at some point to see me, which was wonderful. Later I found out how they had heard about my crash. The Oregon State Police trooper who had arrived at the crash had recognized me since I worked with law enforcement personnel on the child safety seat project and had called my office. Of course, a key identifier was probably the two child safety seats strapped into my car. In fact, I was later told that the emergency service people at first thought children were in the car. They were evidently quite relieved to discover that there were only dolls in the child safety seats.

Ardith, my office manager, got on the phone and was able to find Ray at Oregon State University, and he picked our kids up on the way to the hospital in Portland – about a two hour trip. Aaron was on campus with Ray and Karyn was at Willamette University, which is in Salem on the way to Portland from OSU.

They looked so wonderful, although awfully serious, sad even. I guess the doctor with whom Ray had spoken had scared him, telling him that he better get to the hospital soon because my blood pressure was dropping very low and I had all sorts of injuries. I reassured him with, "Don't worry, I'm a tough old bat." How's that for positive self-image? And in fact, I never thought I was going to die. No, I didn't even get to see a glimpse of the bright light.

Our minister Pastor Gene also arrived and prayed with me. I felt tired, but strangely, at peace. Perhaps I knew that friends and family members were also praying for me; I knew God loved me. I fell asleep. Still no light.

2

The Hospital

"Tough Times Never Last, But Tough People Do!"

Robert Schuller

What happened over the next few days has always been somewhat of a blur of tests, probes, X-rays, a vague memory of going into an MRI tube, signing a permission slip for surgery, and being in and out of consciousness. I was at the mercy of the doctors and nurses and I really did not have my usual questioning, analytical approach to my medical treatment. I was so thankful for the presence of my caring husband, Ray, and I felt alone when he was not there.

Slowly, as I started noticing the tubes, cast, staples, and stitches, I discovered that I had suffered much more serious injuries than I had thought. I learned that I had two collapsed lungs, several broken ribs, a broken right pelvis, a dislocated hip, a shattered knee-cap, a severed patellar (knee) tendon, broken right ankle, and crushed right heel. My friendly truck driver was right: the air bag had probably saved my life, although with critical assistance from the emergency medical technicians and trauma room doctors.

I slept a lot in the ICU, which I imagine was partly the result of the fairly strong doses of morphine they gave me to help with the pain. I was given a button to push after a period of time where I could administer more morphine if I needed it. The nurse seemed perplexed once as she asked me why I was not pressing the button more often. I said I did not want to take too much of it, and that I was doing okay with the amount I was getting. Whatever amount of pain-killer I was getting was keeping me very tired and sleepy. I imagine my body also wanted me to rest so it could heal. I am glad I slept so much because when I was not sleeping, I felt lonely and somewhat frightened in this very foreign and cold environment.

After a couple of days, when I graduated from intensive care to a regular room, I knew I was making progress. My progress was probably due to the fact that I did whatever I was told and I tried to keep a positive attitude. I have always been able to adapt to a wide variety of situations, although none of them were this challenging. Robert Frost put it much more eloquently when he said, "Always fall in with what you're asked to accept. Take what is given and make it over your way."

I imagine that this attitude of dealing with whatever comes at you and working hard to get things to go the way you want started developing in my early years on our farm.

While we lived on a farm with 76 acres, it was not enough acreage to make a living on, so our father had to work in an aluminum plant. Each summer my two brothers and I had to pick berries, and sometimes green beans, to buy school clothes. We would go from picking strawberries, to raspberries, to blackberries, and some years to green beans. I also have a sister who started her work experience the same way, but since she was nine years older, she was graduating from high school and on to the big city of Portland as I joined the berry picking work force. Both my mother and father were of German heritage and had worked hard all of their lives, so we were taught to do the same. Besides, I loved using my hard-earned money to decide what clothes I would buy for school, either through one of the popular catalog stores or on a big bus trip into Portland with my mother. I always saved a portion of my earnings for college and enjoyed keeping "the books" as the interest piled up.

Early on my brothers and I found out that hard work paid off, not just in the berry fields but also in school. Learning came easy for me because I had a wonderful memory. What I read I seemed to retain, and it seemed like I could pick out the important facts that would then appear on the tests. I also worked at it because I knew that I could earn good grades just like I earned good money, for a berry picker anyway. Once I started getting all A's as a freshman in high school, I just did not want to get a B – and I didn't.

I also think a sense of humor helped me cope with hospital life and my recovery as it has all of my life. I developed my sense of humor very early in life since I had two brothers teasing me, and since I was covered with freckles and acted like a true tomboy. I had to have a quick "come-back" for any "put-down" through my elementary and high school years. In fact, I enjoyed joking around so much that, at the National Science Foundation camp I went to after my junior year in high school, I was voted "class clown" as well as winning several other popular categories. Needless to say, I did not tell my mother about this dubious award since she envisioned me hitting the books hard and learning all sorts of higher math, biology, and oceanography. I did learn that I got sea-sick on small boats, so a career in oceanography was out. I was not voted smartest, and in fact, this camp helped me decide not to major in science or math in college but to go into political science instead.

And then there was the time in the eighth grade when I came down with Bell's palsy right as our girls' softball team was about to start the season. I was in contention for the "Best Girl in Sports" award after having played on the basketball and volleyball teams. It was another one of my goals. On the softball team, I was ready to either pitch or play first base. Then while sitting in class one day, I noticed that the right side of my mouth felt numb like I had been to the dentist, but I had not. By the time I got off the school bus at home, I was having trouble closing my right eye-lid. It turned out to be Bell's palsy, which is an inflammation of the facial nerve caused by a virus. The doctor had no solution for the paralysis but said it would be temporary – about a month – and since I was young I would probably have few residual effects. I still cannot blow up a balloon and I do not drink from a straw, but for the most part, he was right.

The doctor gave me some vitamin B-12 shots and essentially told me to cope with it. Unfortunately, he also said, "no sports." I was crushed that I was not going to get to play on the softball team. I was also dreading just going to school in this condition. You can imagine how I needed my sense of humor, not to mention self-confidence, to face my classmates with my mouth drooping. It was hard to talk and there was the occasional problem with drool. The coach let me help keep the softball records so I would still feel a part of the team.

The happy ending was that I was still voted the "Outstanding Girl in Sports" award, although I always wondered if I really had earned it, whether it was fair that I got it. The other part to the happy ending was that later I was allowed to go to California and spend the summer there living with my sister, if I could find a job. With that kind of motivation, I found a job in the mail room of a savings and loan, and I worked there three summers advancing to teller and new account representative. No more berry picking for me!

So what did all this positive attitude, determination, and humor have me doing as I faced the biggest challenge of my life? Let's start with physical therapy, since it was the key to my being able to go home. One of my first physical therapy lessons was on using a walker, the first of many pieces of equipment I would learn to use. To get to the first lesson, I had to first get up out of bed. This was not as easy of a task as one might think. The cast on my leg was very heavy and was covered with a foot to upper-thigh brace. It did not help that I was also very weak at this point. I asked the physical therapist if there was a time limit on getting up – if I used all my time just to get up, could I pass on the rest of the lesson? The physical therapist smiled politely and decided to lift my leg over the edge of the bed so I could sit up. Once my mind convinced my body to take the next step, I was up, although it was not my usual athletic move. I just felt awkward and unsteady, not to mention a little fearful. I held on to the walker for dear life. I told myself I could do this.

While many people use a walker for balance and to avoid falling, I needed to use it so that I could walk on one leg. My "bad" leg was not to have any weight on it. My instructor told me what to do. I was to push the walker forward, and then lift myself enough with my arms so my "good leg" could hop forward to the walker. I took a deep breath, told myself that God was with me, and moved the walker forward with my arms. Then, continuing to hold my "bad leg" off the floor by just a little, I lifted and put my good leg forward and back to the floor. It was not pretty, it was not very far, but I did start to get the hang of it. It was not as much fun as shooting a basket, but it was much more important to my life at this point. After a couple of these steps, I was exhausted and asked for a break. The physical therapist reassured me that I would have many more opportunities to increase my walker skills. I told her I would be waiting with baited breath. But all humor and positive thinking aside, I began to realize that I was not going to be walking without some equipment to help me for quite a while. This realization was hard to accept. I had always cherished my independence and been proud of my athleticism. Now I could not get out of bed by myself, let alone walk on my own. I put that negative thinking out of my mind. I could meet this challenge. I would just work hard and eventually get back to my old self.

Unfortunately, not all my days resulted in some improvement. Sometimes, it seemed that, just as I was taking a step or two forward, I had something happen to stop me in my tracks. For example, the day they thought I could get my chest tubes out, they took me up for an X-ray. Unfortunately, the X-ray revealed some blood around my heart and they rushed me in to do an angiogram. They would not wait for Ray to get there, which was a big disappointment and worried me that maybe something was seriously wrong with my heart. I seemed at the mercy of the doctors, and I was not used to not being in control of my life.

This whole nightmare had nothing to do with any of my dreams or goals; in fact, it appeared to me to be one big roadblock. It was not like I had done anything wrong on

February 3, 1994. Why was this happening to me? I was dejected. I had no one to talk to, and no one was talking to me except when they would tell me what to do or what they were going to do to me.

I later learned that they had suspected bleeding around the heart. The test seemed quite lengthy and was somewhat uncomfortable, as they inserted a needle in a blood vessel in my groin and shot dye to my heart, at least that is how I understood it. I felt very warm, which I was told is normal with this test. I was exhausted afterwards. I had to pass on my physical therapy session that afternoon. I took some control of my life and told the therapist, "No, I am too tired to try today." She must have been able to tell that I was truly exhausted, or maybe she was not interested in arguing. Regardless, she did not pursue the lesson. I needed time to try to relax and figure out what was happening to me.

I was so relieved when Ray arrived and I told him about the test and how helpless I felt. He held my hand and said he would find out the results. He knew what to say to calm and reassure me. The doctors always seemed reluctant to talk to me. Ray reported that they told him that while there was a little blood near the heart, my heart was fine. The bleeding had probably been caused by my broken ribs, but was limited and not problematic. The good news was very welcome.

Ray would go to church when I was in the hospital to let our congregation know how I was doing. He also needed his spirit nourished and his hope encouraged. Then he would lift my spirits as he told me how everyone cared about how I was doing. It helped to know that many people were praying for me. I prayed too for God's continued presence in my life and for His support and strength to do what I needed to in order to walk again.

I am not sure of the order of some of my improvements and what seemed like accomplishments to me, but the catheter came out next, I think, and I advanced to the commode next to the bed. Unfortunately, this step always required the assistance of a nurse due to my inability to lift my heavy right leg (heavy, of course, only due to the cast). The chest tubes came out as my lungs re-inflated, and the angiogram showed no damage to the heart. I was also always blowing into a contraption (a spirometer) that was supposed to indicate my increase in lung capacity, later identified as the pulmonary function test. There was this small ball that was supposed to go up to a high number if I blew hard enough. Not only was this test not easy for me to do, but I was constantly asked by nurses how close I was getting to their goal for me. This may sound like I was losing my sense of humor; it's just that I always got the feeling that this was an area where the nurses did not think I was trying often and hard enough. It seemed like it took a lot of energy. It certainly was not easy for me. They always looked disappointed when I demonstrated my progress with what I thought was my best effort. In retrospect, they were probably right to keep bugging me about it, but it just seemed more important to me to use my limited energy to work on getting up, not blowing in a bottle. I have always liked to set my own goals, and walking again was my highest priority.

As my head cleared, meaning the drugs were cut back, I was now ready and able to engage my doctors, who did not seem to want to stay in the room very long. They complimented me on my very fast progress, but were very vague about my foot injury and, specifically, about how long it would be before I would walk unassisted. They concentrated their attention on my hip and were very clear that it would need to heal first, and that would take about six weeks. I could feel the many staples running down my right hip and thigh – all 12 inches of them – which is where they inserted a plate to hold my hip together. The heel injury, which no one would explain to me and I could not see because of the cast from foot to knee, would be addressed later. In any event, I was told that I would not be putting weight on that leg, hip, and foot for at least three months!

Oregon Health Sciences University is a teaching hospital, so there was at least one foul up on my foot. Not that teaching hospitals have to have foul ups, but you do receive some care from people who are not doctors yet. My ankle had been casted early on, and then one day I was sent down to a department to have a leg brace fitted. Somewhere along the line someone decided to remove the cast and just let the brace do the job, evidently without asking the doctor in charge (surely there was one in charge) if that change was okay. When the doctor who seemed to be in charge saw what had happened the next morning, he was not happy and quickly ordered the cast put back on. Since the cast was put on right away, I am quite sure the doctor in charge had spoken. I did try to keep my sense of humor through it all, but I was tested. I thought I might get some perky color for my cast, but the technician or intern had white and that was what I got.

Once I was starting to feel good and my mind (or so I thought) was working pretty good, I started phoning some of my clients. They probably thought my mind was not working since I was not even home from the hospital yet. I just did not want to hurt their projects or lose their business. What I thought I could do from my hospital bed I really do not know, but it was a relief to hear how supportive and caring they were. They told me not to worry, to just get better. But I wanted them to know that I would not let this "incident" hold me back for very long.

I look back on this now and wonder if other people get as obsessed with their work as I was. When bad things happen, there can be some good outcomes. One for me was getting a more balanced approach to life — and a greater appreciation for family, friends, nature, time, and the beauty in life. I know, sounds pretty corny, but it has been life enriching. I will talk about the good things that came out of all of this later.

As I got better on the walker and the tests gave the doctors reason to believe that I could now be treated in outpatient mode, I was told I could go home. I had been in the hospital only ten days. The doctors were very impressed with my very fast improvement – or so they told me. They even mentioned that I would be a candidate for the "Rose Award" if it were not for the fact that these awards were only given to staff for exemplary effort/improvement. I'm not sure that was the exact name of the award, but you got a pin in the shape of a rose. For the non-Oregonian, Portland is known for its roses and the annual Rose Festival, hence the choice of the award name. Could it be that I was even an overachiever in the hospital? I certainly did not look or feel like an overachiever.

I certainly wanted to go home, but I am not sure how the doctors determined that I was ready. I guess getting all of my tubes removed was a good indication. I was now able with nurse assistance to get up and urinate in the commode by my bed.

However, there were some things that should have raised a few doubts about my readiness to leave the hospital. Even when I exerted all my energy to breathe deeply, my lungs could not get the floating ball up to the mark that they wanted. Even more important, as I was to discover, was the fact that I had not had a bowel movement before leaving the hospital.

Complicating my move home was the fact that the hospital had a new social worker who was supposed to help me with the transition and who was ill-prepared to do that.

She was new to her position – bad timing for me. Having never been in this situation before, I had no idea what sort of equipment and support I would need at home to continue my healing. It was also all new for Ray, who I am sure was emotionally drained and tired, and not up to his usual fact-finding self. But I was anxious to go home. Being in a hospital was not where I wanted to be. I had no control and no privacy. Doctors and nurses decided what I would do, when, and how. I was even weighed like a sack of beans. It seemed I was only able to do what I was told to do in the hospital. There was little meaningful conversation and certainly no hugs. I could certainly see that people who do not think they have any control over their lives could easily become depressed. But I told myself that once I got home, everything would be fine.

The doctors said I could go home; I wanted to go home; so I went home. Much to my surprise, I was sent home in a wheelchair riding high in the back of a van, feeling very vulnerable. I had to go by myself, which added to my uneasiness. My wheelchair added to my fear as I had to sit in one with the back tilted slightly back as I was not to sit at a ninety degree angle due to my hip injuries. In addition, my right leg was held up and extended out in front on a leg rest. I knew the wheelchair was attached to a certain extent to the floor of the van, but it moved back and forth some as the van sped down the freeway. I am so thankful that we made it home without incident. I am not sure how many prayers I said. I think my eyes were wide open only about half of the time – kind of like riding a roller coaster. I was just too scared to watch the whole trip home to safety.

Once home, we had to figure out how to get me into the house. Not that I did any of the figuring. We have a ranch-style house and it takes two steps up to get into the house. Funny, I had never really paid any attention to those steps before now. It was determined that there was only one way to get me inside. I had to be lifted in the wheelchair into the house. This was not all that easy given my extended leg and my non-petite size: 5 feet 9 inches and slightly overweight (more than 100 and less than 200 pounds – you didn't really think I would be exact, did you?).

I was so excited to be going home and then to get home safely. I did not even have a clue of the challenges yet to be faced.

3

Marooned in the Family Room

"I always say, dare to struggle, dare to grin."

Wavy Gravy

I entered the family room, which is just inside the carport door, and saw the roll-away bed Ray had put in the place where the sofa had been. It seemed an ideal spot for me to be; right by the window with a nice view of our Japanese maple, rhododendrons, and other trees and shrubs. And also with a direct view of the television since this was our television-watching room. I was greeted by our kids, Aaron and Karyn, and wheeled over to my new bed. By their facial expressions I could tell they were happy to see me, but also a little apprehensive.

Fortunately, this room's floor was vinyl, which I would truly come to appreciate. The smooth surface made using the wheelchair and other assist equipment much easier than if the floor had been carpeted. And to think that I had often hinted at how much warmer that floor and room would be if we had carpet in it.

Next came the big move into the bed. Ray undid the wheelchair's leg support and helped me up and then down – way down – into bed. It was not an easy transfer as the bed was so low compared to my bed at the hospital – and way too soft. It did not feel right. I have always preferred a stiffer mattress, but especially at this time, I really needed the support. Ray positioned some pillows to keep me from lying flat – a requirement for my hip. More pillows went under my right foot and leg to keep it elevated. We were doing our best to follow doctors' orders – and it felt better to me.

I noticed immediately that Ray had rearranged the furniture rather dramatically. The sofa and chairs were all pushed back against the walls. And they were all jammed together so that my bed could be next to the wall with the big window. That was usually where our sofa was. This was done to allow plenty of room for moving with my walker and to allow for more room to move in soon-to-come equipment and, of course, the hospital bed. All the furniture was now covered with blankets. Ray has always been very practical – a true engineer. The room was not going to win any "Good Housekeeping" awards, but it was just the way it needed to be for me.

It became very clear to me why a hospital bed was needed. I could not get comfortable in the roll-away. And to think this was the bed we so generously gave our house guests to sleep on. It was too soft and could not be adjusted so I could sit up. The pillows, while helpful, just did not provide enough support. It was also hard to keep them in the right place or even on the bed. Ray had to research companies that rented hospital beds and that would deliver out where we lived (about 25 miles from Portland and 8 miles from Oregon City), since the hospital social worker had not been at all helpful with this. Maybe if we had known to ask what kind of special furniture I would need for my recovery at home – and where to get it – my adjustment to life at home would have gone much smoother.

For example, it quickly became clear that I also needed a portable commode – one that could sit by the bed. I could not get up by myself, and once up, I could not sit on a regular toilet seat. It was too low. Also, the toilet I would eventually use was in a bathroom that had a narrow hallway access, and I could not maneuver the walker and my leg to successfully get to the target. Needless to say, that first night, using a bedpan was extremely uncomfortable and inadequate. I am sure Ray would agree. More than enough said!

The bed and commode arrived two days later and I was ecstatic. I mean the event wasn't as big as winning the lottery would be, but it was big to me and even more so to Ray. The increase in comfort was so appreciated, and while it was still not easy to use a commode without any privacy or without help to get to it, it sure beat the bedpan. With the arrival of the hospital bed, I was able to sit and sleep with my back at an angle, which was required until my hip and pelvis healed, and it provided needed support. I still used a big pillow to elevate my foot, which helped with pain and swelling.

As you can deduce from this accumulation of equipment, I was completely dependent on others for my care. Ray immediately took a leave of absence from Oregon State University and his PhD program. He slept for the first few weeks on the sofa near my bed so he could get up and help me get up to use the commode during the night. He washed me and cooked for me and even planted some flowers in a flowerbox for me to see outside my window.

Actually, he did not have to do a lot of cooking as the members of our church, Carus United Methodist Church, brought a meal each day. They were really terrific and when they brought a meal, it was usually enough for two meals. I do not know what it is, but Methodists seem to be especially good cooks, not to mention good eaters.

Our pastor also continued to visit regularly. Pastor Gene is a short, graying man with a ready smile and a wonderful hearty laugh. His visits were always light and enjoyable. Pastor Gene kept Ray company too, especially when I was in the hospital. He accompanied him to the wrecking yard where my car was and helped him deal with seeing the mangled auto body and retrieving what he wanted from the trunk. His words for me were always very positive and encouraging, and I am so glad he was our pastor.

Through the years, I have noticed that pastors have different strengths that they bring to their ministry. Some are very spiritual and inspirational in their sermons and really are effective in the church service itself. However, some of the pastors I have had who have these strengths, are not as good at the pastoral care part of their ministry. By this I mean, they are not as strong at interpersonal relations – visiting those who are sick, emotionally hurting, shut-in, or otherwise in need. Other pastors have been so caring in all of their actions and words but not so strong in sermons. To me, Pastor Gene's sermons were more on the folksy side as opposed to being highly spiritual or inspirational, but he was great at pastoral care. He just seemed to know what to say to a person to make them feel better or to let them know that he had heard your concern. Sometimes, he did not even say that much, but he was there. For example, he noticed that I had no place by my hospital bed to put the radio or books I was reading – or anything else – so he took Ray to the church bazaar because he had spotted the perfect table. It was high and long with a few slots for smaller things – and in great condition. It was put to good use immediately. On it went my radio, reading materials, client files (just in case), and anything else. That kept my eating tray/table free for the full meal deal.

My faith has strengthened over a long period of time. I have attended Methodist churches for many years, although I was active in the Presbyterian Church in my younger years in Sandy. My parents did not attend church, but my father took us every Sunday to Sunday school. In many respects, I attended church when I was young because it provided a very positive social involvement. I liked the other kids who went to this church, and I enjoyed many positive youth experiences during my participation. But these activities did not get me closer to God. However, I did pray to God – not just the prayers we are taught as children such as "Now I lay me down to sleep …" I prayed that my father would live until we kids were old enough to take care of my mom. Dad was seventeen years older than Mom, and that was always a concern of mine that I asked God to handle.

I did not have the dramatic moment where I knew I had turned my life over to God. But I did know somehow that God was with me, and certainly my childhood was blessed. I also received a wonderful set of values that I cherish and try to live by to this day.

During my college years, my faith took a back seat to my social life and learning. I just did not find time for meditation or going to church on a regular basis. I mean socializing and studying were a full-time job. Oh, I made it to church a few times and I did pray occasionally, but other activities were clearly priorities. I came back to the church after marriage and particularly, after having children.

On the day of the crash (C-Day), my faith was strong, but it would only become more vital and more spiritual. Our family had attended the same small community church for years. Ray and I had served on just about every committee and at the time of my crash, I had been the chair of the Administrative Council for years. I was also teaching an adult Sunday school class.

Despite my relatively strong faith, I was not always sure of the benefits of prayer in my pre-crash days. It seemed like a lot of times what I prayed for just did not happen, particularly when people died. But now I discovered that when you know that people are praying for you, you know people care. Somehow it provided me with encouragement and hope. I, of course, also prayed, and I prayed for strength and courage and for help with pain. Those prayers made me feel closer to God, and I tried to listen back for a response. This was the first time I did that. I mean, I had the time to really just relax after prayer. I was not in church and needing to go on to a hymn or needing to go home. When I took that time to be quiet and listen, I truly felt closer to God and to His comforting and love.

My days were less than exciting, but then I did not have the energy for exciting. I mostly read, listened to the radio, or watched TV – actually, I was excited to get to see the "March to the Final Four" as I enjoy college basketball but had never had, or taken, the time to watch the games. But daytime TV, during most of the time, was not my cup of tea. I preferred sleeping, reading, or listening to public radio. Unfortunately, I found it difficult to stop thinking that I was getting behind at work. Would clients start leaving or canceling contracts? It was frustrating to realize that I really could not do much of anything. Of course, realizing it and accepting it were two different things.

For the most part, the medications stemmed the pain. Of course, they were very strong to start with. In fact, Ray had to drive back up to the hospital in Portland to get refills as they would not, perhaps could not, write a prescription for this type of narcotic. We did not know this was going to be the case, so once I even ran out of medication before Ray could drive to the hospital, a 45 minute drive each way at non-commute times. He could not leave me until someone else was able to come and stay with me.

If only we had known in the hospital to ask not just where I should get my prescription filled, but also any side effects to watch for. Unfortunately, these high-powered drugs cause constipation, of which I developed a royal case. Now, one might not think this a very serious thing when compared to my other problems, but it caused me a great deal of pain. In fact, I still have indentations on my arms from where I pressed down on the arms of the commode when trying to endure the pain of attempting to have a bowel movement. I also developed a royal case of hemorrhoids, which also had to be treated by my caregiver. Did I have lucky caregivers, or what?

We did not know which of my doctors to call regarding this development. Yes, another one of those questions I will ask before leaving the hospital in the future. Friends recommended all sorts of remedies for the constipation –

prune juice, castor oil, Citrucel — and finally, it happened. And it happened in a big way. And I couldn't clean myself. That was one of the most humiliating feelings I think there can be. This was especially hard for one who had been raised to be independent and self-reliant. There are just some things you want to do for yourself in private. I certainly felt like I was getting an overdose of humbling experiences.

Because of the medications — at least that is what I would like to think was the cause — I had a hard time concentrating on and therefore enjoying my usual reading subjects, biographies and history. A friend from church brought me a book she had enjoyed, and at first I thought it kind of beneath my Stanford-groomed genius but decided to give it a try one day. I ended up eventually reading the whole Mitford (name of the fictional small southern town in which these stories unfold) series by Jan Karon. They were light and reminded me somewhat of the small town in which I had attended elementary and high school. They also have a strong faith basis, which I found reassuring and comforting. I needed positive stories where everything worked out for the best.

I was visited by a member of the Clackamas County sheriff's crash reconstruction team. It was not a social visit. The officer knew of my traffic safety work and was sympathetic, but also very business-like. They, along with the Oregon State Police, had investigated my crash. I learned that the police had closed the highway for about two hours after my crash, which is the normal procedure when they think someone has been killed. Their crash investigation team found that I was going about 50 mph and the other driver between 55 and 65 mph. With the resulting force of the impact of our two vehicles, one can see why the police thought someone might not survive. In fact, it was amazing that we both survived. The woman who hit me was driving with an expired license and was found to be driving "too fast for conditions." The sheriff's deputy was not going to cite her, however, because she had a head trauma and would be in the hospital or other facility for an unknown amount of time. While I thought I had been pretty alert at the time of the crash, the officer told me details that I did not see. For example, I did not see the driver of the pickup fly through her windshield and pass in front of my windshield.

At that point, I am not sure how I felt about the driver who had put me through all this pain and turned my life upside down. Strangely enough, I did not feel animosity. That is not to say I did not recognize that she had been responsible for the crash. I really did not think about her at all at this point. I have always had a stronger focus on the present and future. At this point in my life, the past was water over the dam. I had to concentrate on me and getting back to my life. I wanted to think positive thoughts about getting better, and not to spend any precious energy looking back and thinking "if only." Little did I know that her decision to drive too fast would also cause Ray and me all sorts of legal and financial hassles with my umbrella and disability insurance companies. "Getting back to my life" would prove to be quite the challenge.

One of the volunteer firemen who had been on the scene of my crash and went with me in the ambulance found out my phone number and called to say how happy he was to learn that I had lived; that he had rescued many who did not. This caring attitude from someone I did not really know was very touching. From my viewpoint, very special people become emergency service personnel.

I learned after the crash that the stretch of Highway 26 where my crash happened had for some time been called "Blood Alley" by local emergency responder personnel. It was a stretch that has had more than its share of head-on crashes, many of them fatal. The Oregon Department of Transportation has now installed, in a two mile section of this area, a high-tension cable barrier in the median to prevent vehicles from crossing over into oncoming traffic. While this is experimental as the median is so narrow, I am hopeful that future crashes may be prevented and sad that so many had to suffer and die before action was taken.

There were many more humbling experiences ahead for me after settling into my special corner of the house. After a couple of weeks, I had encouraged Ray to go sleep in our bed so he would get a good night's rest. Since our bedroom was at the opposite end of the house, he would only agree if I would ring a bell he had put by my bed if I needed to get up to go to the bathroom. Well, one night I thought I could handle getting to the commode by myself since I had gotten a little more strength in my leg. With my best effort I managed to get up, but as I reached for the walker I lost my balance. At least I was coordinated enough to direct my fall onto my good hip. But of course, I could not get up off the floor, so I had to call for Ray, who had already started coming based on the noise created by my non-soft landing. Needless to say, Ray would not go back to sleeping in the bedroom until I had proven myself "commode able."

Because of my physical limitations, I couldn't travel easily and yet, I had outpatient appointments to go to. We — read that Ray — called a cab company that was supposed to transport people with disabilities, but since we didn't have a wheelchair yet, I had to lie on the back seat, but with my back at an angle up against one of the doors. After all my work in traffic safety, I was appalled that I was letting myself be transported this way, but at that point, what choice did I have? I worried the whole way there, even with the strong meds at work in my body.

Whenever we went to the hospital, Ray always had to find a wheelchair that would recline slightly and that had a leg support. Fortunately, he was always able to find one and get me out of that cab. Unfortunately the first time we went to the hospital, I had to go to the bathroom by the time Ray got the wheelchair. By the time we got to the bathroom, I did not have the strength to get up on my good leg fast enough and I wet myself all over. Ray cleaned me up the best he could. It was all I could do to keep from crying. What a low point in my life. It was not possible to activate my sense of humor at that moment.

My next appointment went well (no bathroom mishap), although they took the cast off to look at the ankle to see if the gash was healing, and then put a new cast back on. Two days later, we were back at the hospital getting the cast split as my leg had swollen and the cast was too tight. Nothing helped with the pain. What an exhausting couple of days, and I can only imagine the frustration Ray was feeling. At least the splitting of the cast relieved the pain and I could sleep again.

Every outing sapped any strength I had. After one of these hospital visits, Bonnie, a friend from church who was a nurse, happened to stop by to visit and give me a massage and wash my hair. That might seem like such a minor thing, but to me it was the high point of the day and helped me relax.

I also received comfort from an unexpected source at random times during the day and night. Our cat would join me on the bed and seemed to know that he could not lay on me, but anywhere next to me was just fine; in fact, was quite welcome. Sox was actually our son Aaron's cat, but since he was away in college, Ray and I took over as his guardians. We may have only partially appreciated Sox before he showed his true contributions; I mean he was a wonderful companion, but he also was a very quick and skilled hunter. Our lawn, while not always green, never had gopher or mole holes until Sox died at the ripe old age of 14.

I gave up trying to do any work for the time being. My office administrator, Ardith, came by to visit and update me on what was happening with our clients. Everyone was being very understanding and was willing to wait for future work. All small business owners should have such a competent, caring, and loyal employee as Ardith. I doubt that she even reported all the hours she worked during my absence. I know she calmed all the clients' concerns as she certainly always calmed mine.

Once the doctor proclaimed that my hip and pelvis were sufficiently healed, although the steel plate would remain in the hip, I was pronounced ready for in-home physical therapy. This was about six weeks after C-Day (crash day). I had no idea what I was in for. I pictured some wonderful massage therapy. It turned out that I had lost all range of motion in my right knee. Knee "range of motion," as I soon learned, is the arc your lower leg makes as you bring the foot of your extended leg as far back to the underside of your thigh as possible. It is measured in degrees from the straight extended leg. Zero is not good.

My knee had no degrees of motion; it did not bend one iota. Not only had it not been moved while the hip and pelvis were healing, but it was also healing itself and forming scar tissue. All the bones in the shattered kneecap had grown back together. The X-ray just amazed me, as I could see all the little lines like countries on a map where the pieces had come back together to form the continent. The severed tendon had also healed. The doctor stated very matter-of-factly, "So now we have to work on regaining range of motion in your knee." Sounds so simple and straightforward. Unfortunately, it meant cracking up all the scar tissue that had formed by taking my lower leg and bending it back and forth at the knee. Crunch. Crunch. Crunch. The sound of scar tissue cracking and breaking apart was almost as bad as the pain.

The in-home health nurse came twice a week and did this "therapy," and I cannot say that I looked forward to seeing her. This physical therapist was all business. No small talk, jokes, or casual conversation. She got right to work on this truly painful process. I felt accomplished for every degree of motion attained. I only wished I had had ear plugs so that I would not have had to hear the cracking sounds. They only seemed to emphasize the shots of pain. Afterwards came the ice packs, and while the first couple of packs were a shock to my system, they were much appreciated – meaning, they helped the pain big time. Ice was my friend from then on.

In between sessions with the physical therapist, I was to do exercises, which I did as I could. The physical therapist insisted after a while that the exercises were too easy for me and requested, in a very convincing way, that Ray buy weights to attach to my arms and legs. Now I have always loved sports, especially competitive sports, but I have never loved exercises – they just always seemed so boring and delayed getting to the game where the real fun was to be had. However, I did what I was told and I did not complain (out loud anyway) – that's the way I was brought up. Are all physical therapists so motivational? Intimidation is motivating at times. But so too was my strong desire to get this rehabilitation behind me and get back to my life.

Now, you may think that my life at home confined to a bed and dependent on my family and friends for most of my daily activities of living would truly be a drag. But in some ways it was relaxing – except for the intrusion of some mighty powerful pain, it was somewhat like a vacation. I mean since there was no working, no cooking, and no cleaning, I had time to become more introspective. I learned that quiet could be enjoyable and that patience could be increased. Probably most important, I felt safe there. The only parts of a true vacation that were missing: fun, getting out to see new places and things, feeling rejuvenated, not having any cares, and being able to take care of myself and my family. Try as I might, I also could not stop worrying about getting behind on my work projects. Maybe "vacation" is just not the right word.

And there were some high points, like our 25th wedding anniversary. By this point, June 21, 1994, I was able to go short distances on crutches, so our children fixed a barbeque for Ray and me and we sat on our deck. Lest you be thinking, wow, do they know how to pull out all the stops – for me this was a wonderful day, my family together, wonderful food, champagne (I know I was not to be having alcohol with my meds, but this one exception was not reported), and even sunshine (yes, in Oregon). Ray and I promised each other that we would add to the celebrations later with trips.

Another high point was getting to take baths, which did not happen for several months. This took a lot of work on Ray's behalf again. He had to attach a hand-held shower unit with hose to our shower head and buy a shower bench. Until I got the cast off of my leg, I had to rest my right leg on the top of the side of the tub, so my back was facing the faucet. But ohhhh did that hot water and soap feel good. And when the cast finally came off, my poor calf had shriveled up and was covered with long hair. I could believe that we humans are related to the monkey. But at least I could now get both legs into the bath tub and could wash my own hair. Whoever said we take even little things for granted sure knew what she was talking about.

In looking back at the challenges we faced when I returned home, it became clear that we had learned the hard way that our lives would have been a whole lot easier if we had known to ask these questions before we left the hospital:

- What should I expect as far as pain is concerned?
- If I have questions about pain or other concerns, whom do I call? I had multiple doctors.

- Who will refill my prescriptions? It would have been very helpful to know that Ray would need to drive back up to the hospital to get my narcotic prescription refilled.
- With whom will I have a follow-up appointment and when?
- How can I get transportation for my follow-up appointments?
- What kind of special equipment or furniture do I need at home? Where can I get it?
- What types of things (pain, diarrhea, constipation, bleeding) should I be concerned about?
- How can I wash my hair?
- Do I have any diet restrictions?

Of course, knowing the questions to ask now still depends on the hospital having social workers and other health care providers who know the answers and can help you. I knew I would be prepared next time, although I was hoping to avoid any next time.

4

Meet the Family Caregivers

*"Sometimes our light goes out but is blown
into flame by another human being.
Each of us owes deepest thanks to those
who have rekindled this light."*

Albert Schweitzer

As I was healing physically, Ray decided that I really should get out of the house some. My engineer husband had a psychologist's side to him. I wanted to resist this — not his psych side, but getting out. It just seemed like it would take too much energy, and I wasn't sure I would feel safe. I was quite comfortable in my bed and in my routine. I just did not want to get re-hurt some way. I know that probably sounds kind of wacky, but I wanted nothing more than to get better and get back to my "normal" life. Going outside my safe environment seemed risky and a little frightening.

Well, Ray can be persuasive and I agreed to give it a try. After all he had gone to the trouble of renting a wheelchair that met all of my needs. The wheelchair joined our growing arsenal of special needs equipment: walker, hospital bed, a toilet seat raiser, a bathtub chair, a bed table that adjusted so I could eat off of it or put small things on it, and a commode. The hospital had given me those completely worthless long-handled pincers that you are supposed to use to pull your socks on with. I wonder if anyone really uses those. I certainly was not going to be able to give them a try for quite a while, and in fact, I never did use them. These pincers and the walker were the hospital's total contributions to my home adjustment.

This first trip out "for fun" was not exactly a great success. First, I had to put on some "going out" clothes. My wardrobe at this time consisted of sweats with the right leg cut open up to the middle of the thigh, and one of my nice pants suits with the same alteration. These alterations were necessary to get pants over the cast and brace on my right leg. After choosing my outfit – this process has never taken so little time: let me see, sweats or no sweats? – Ray helped me dress and get into the wheelchair.

The next truly daunting task was getting into the SUV. Ray had made a ramp to get in and out of the house at the door to "my room." That put me right in the carport where our vehicle was parked. So getting to the SUV, a Mazda Navajo was a piece of cake. I cannot say the same thing for getting into it. At this point, my leg still could not bend much, so Ray put the seat back as far as it would go and reclined it as far as it would go. I got my rear end as far back up on the seat as I could, pushing down on the console for support and pushing up with my good leg from the floor. Crash! I broke off part of the console. I thought about calling the outing off right then and there, but I was determined not to let Ray down. I took a deep breath and kept trying to get my back further into the car so there would be room for my leg to wedge into the car. I eventually got my leg in. It was not a comfortable feeling, but I was all inside of the car.

Since it was still daylight, we went to the mall. Getting out of the vehicle was easier (remember, everything is relative), now that I knew the angles. At least I did not break off any more of the console. Once in the wheelchair, I again felt the pangs of fear. My "bad" leg was straight out in front of me on the wheelchair's extension for legs that needed to be elevated. I could just imagine someone not seeing me and running into my leg. But I knew Ray would be careful, and I was not going to turn back after making it this far. As it turned out, Ray was very good at watching for and avoiding possible collisions. We escaped with only one bump and it was minor.

I got a real education that afternoon on what it feels like to have a disability. All of the clerks ignored me and talked only to Ray. I decided to look for a new watch since the one I was wearing on C-Day did not turn up in the hospital. I felt like a non-person, or at least one who could not possibly make decisions if I were in a wheelchair. It is hard to describe how I felt other than to say that it was a real eye-opener to being treated differently just because I was in a wheelchair. This episode attacked my sense of self-worth and self-confidence just when I was having a hard enough time with my complete dependence on others. But I was determined not to let it get me down for long; I needed all my energies focused on getting better.

While I was glad to get home and I was very tired, I had to admit it had been good to get outside my room and feel a part of the world again. While I had been ignored and treated disrespectfully by some in that world, I knew that I had learned an important lesson. I knew that I would always treat a person with disabilities with respect and as I would any other person. Eventually, I would even get the opportunity to be an advocate for people with disabilities. And an immediate improvement in my life resulted from the outing: there would be no more nerve-wracking cab rides to the hospital! I could ride in our SUV and use a safety belt.

One day Ray asked if I would like to see where he was working in the house. He was working on his research project for his PhD in computer science during most days when I was sleeping or things were under control. He wanted to be ready to go back to school when I no longer was dependent on him. I certainly was curious to see what he had set up for himself. The wheelchair did not have much clearance going down our hallway, but we made it to the entry of the sunken living room where my mouth dropped open — it might have hit my lap — in utter shock. My living room was covered in sheets and books, and computer cables went through holes drilled in the walls! When Ray saw my reaction, I was quickly reassured that this was just temporary – until I recovered and he could get back to school. Oh yes, and he promised to fill in the holes. I think this may have been his way of inspiring me to keep working hard on my exercises – it worked big time.

It became clear that Ray needed some respite from the constant demands of caregiving. I am not saying that I was demanding, but it cannot be easy to have to be responsible for feeding, cleaning, dressing – well, every activity of daily living of another person (some details are better left undescribed). Fortunately, a dear friend from our church, Marie, volunteered to do this once a week. It gave Ray a much needed break and gave me some additional companionship. I was fortunate to have such a caring and compassionate friend. She made it much easier to let her do and see me do activities of daily living that are very private.

Our daughter, Karyn, also came as much as she could to take care of me. Talk about reversal of roles. It meant so much to have her there, but wasn't I supposed to be taking care of her? I know it was not easy for her. She was a junior at Willamette (Wil-lam-ette for you non-northwesterners) University and president of her sorority, and here she was cleaning me up. I was so lucky that she had not wanted to go too far from home for college. Willamette is about an hour from our home. She was a natural at showing care and listening to how I felt about things. I was not surprised that after graduating from Willamette, she went to Portland State University and earned a Master of Social

Work. Her profession is providing therapy for children and their families. In addition, I could tell even then that she would be a wonderful mother, and since the birth of her first child, Noah, in May 2006, she proves me right every day. And now, Clara has joined the family in August 2008. I thought I was patient in my younger years, but she is the real deal. She is an exceptional daughter!

I think I should tell you a little more about the special problem-solver and primary caregiver of mine since Ray was such an integral part of my recovery, as well as my life. I think this will be helpful in explaining how our relationship not only survived my ordeal, but strengthened.

I met Ray at Stanford University. It is amazing that two people from such similar backgrounds and so different from the vast majority of students at Stanford would meet on a campus as big as Stanford's. We were both there on scholarships and came from rural areas. Ray came from Greenacres, Washington. Yes, there is a real Greenacres, although it is a lot different from the Green Acres in the TV show. Greenacres is located in the Spokane Valley, not far from the Idaho border.

From Ray's childhood pictures, I would have to say that he was a tall scrawny kid with prominent ears. He and his two brothers were taught to work hard and did so on the family mink ranch. He had the scars to prove it, as those animals are vicious. His parents and his faith gave him a strong sense of right and wrong. His parents encouraged his curiosity and intellectual inquiries. He had a basement chemistry room where he concocted all sorts of experiments, which resulted in strange smells drifting upstairs and lights flickering. He and his brothers even made root beer until a bottle exploded and mouse parts were sprayed all over the kitchen. That was a little too much experimentation even for his supportive parents.

His hard work and determination resulted in his earning the Eagle Scout rank in Boy Scouts and very good grades in school. He got into Stanford because of very high SAT scores (not like me). While in high school, he won a big science award for his project that involved shooting a stream of electricity through a hard hat he wore (no kidding). I believe it was an effort to show if learning could increase through electrical stimulation. You can imagine how telling that story just never grows old in our family.

We met as a result of both having attended the Stanford-in-Austria campus. He went eighteen months before me, but his best friend and roommate, Mike, went when I did. Upon returning to the Stanford campus, Mike held a gluhwein (hot spiced wine) party for a few of us from Austria IV and there was Ray. I thought he was very attractive. He was now 6'5" and about 180 pounds. His hair was light brown, even blond during the summer. His ears were no longer prominent. He had a quick wit and great sense of humor, and I liked that he was so smart.

We proceeded to have a lot of fun on campus as well as in San Francisco. He graduated in 1968 with a BS in Electrical Engineering (with honors) but stayed and got his masters in 1969, which is when I graduated (okay, not with honors but a solid B average). We married that June.

Ray and I lived in Maryland for four years while LTJG Liere taught at the Navy's Nuclear Power School. I worked in the office of an auto auction business. We enjoyed the rural setting and we had our two wonderful children while living there. After he satisfied his service obligation, we returned to the West Coast where Ray has since pursued a career in computer science. And I discovered what profession I wanted to pursue in addition to being a mother.

After I got my Master of Public Administration in June, 1979, I started work for the Clackamas County Community Development Department. I wanted to work in programs that helped communities and low-income people. It was a great place to start. I also hired a house cleaner once a week so I could spend more home time with Ray and the kids.

Ray started Vantage Consulting and Research in 1983 and I joined full time in 1985. I had gone as far as I was going to in the agency I was working in, the Social Services Division. I was the Deputy Director for the Community Action Agency, the side of the Social Services Division that provided services to low-income people. I was ready for new challenges and thought I could help Ray develop Vantage.

I got involved in the local Chamber of Commerce and became its first woman president. I also started consulting with government and nonprofit organizations. I had not really planned on doing my own consulting, but when people approached me I was very excited about continuing to work in areas where I thought I could make a contribution. Ray landed one of the first Small Business Innovative Research contracts in Clackamas County.

By 1990, my consulting work had become the mainstay of the business, as Ray was having difficulty getting federal research contracts because he did not have a PhD. He was also the only technical person on our staff. It had always been one of his goals to get a PhD, and this seemed like a good time to pursue it. I mean why not have him join Aaron and Karyn as college students?

Unfortunately, here we were, three years later facing a new challenge together, before he could earn his doctorate. This was not the learning experience he chose, but he dove into my problems full time. I cannot imagine how hard that was for him. He did not have any training in caregiving; he did not know the resource agencies. He did not know the questions to ask until we were in the middle of a problem. He wanted to be going to school. C-Day was not just a life-changer for me, it affected my whole family.

Because I could not know what Ray and Karyn thought as their lives took a major detour in order to help me, I have asked each of them to describe how they felt during this time.

Karyn had this to say:

I was grateful to be a caregiver to Mom, especially after what I felt and thought the day of the crash. Based on my dad's trembling voice when he phoned me at college to say Mom was in the emergency room, the gloomy look on the doctors' faces who met with us, and the sympathetic looks from the hospital staff, I was not sure what was going to happen that day but it did not seem optimistic. When I first got to see Mom after her multiple surgeries, I was physically nauseous with fear and the unknown of what was to come and yet cautiously relieved that Mom was still here. I heard a quote at a conference to the effect of, "Mothers are a daughter's compass in life. Therefore, losing a mother feels like you've lost your direction in life." This quote continues to resonate with me and to some degree encapsulates my feelings for Mom.

I think I was more worried about Mom feeling self-conscious, embarrassed, or sad while I was helping care for her than I was focused on my own feelings. I remember being fairly anxious the majority of the time — wondering how Mom was doing while I was back on campus during the week and certainly concerned for her health when I was home. One very clear memory is when Mom would need Dad or me in the middle of the night. She would ring a bell since we might not hear her otherwise. I remember walking down the long hallway, wondering what was wrong ... too much pain, a fall, or something else that might be too much for us to handle this time. I still cringe when I hear that bell ring.

I never questioned whether I wanted to help out; it seemed the natural thing to do and I only wished I had more time to give and could lift my mom's spirits more. I think Mom protected me from a fair amount of what she was feeling and I certainly have learned more about her and her experience from reading this book. So really, Mom was still being a caregiver to her daughter, still protecting me when I was supposed to be helping her. After you read this book you will realize what an amazing person my mom is, so why would I ever question giving as much time as I could to care for her?

Ray had this to say:

Helen wanted me to describe how I felt. Initially I was in shock at the magnitude of Helen's injuries, and I feared that we would lose her. I prayed a lot, and I even bargained with God. When she reached the point where it was fairly certain that she would live, what rejoicing there was! But her injuries were major, and she would need a lot of care, for quite a while. It never occurred to me not to be her caregiver. We love each other.

Through the months, there were lots of things that I learned — often the hard way. There ought to be a manual! I often felt like I was walking on moss-covered rocks. There were so many things that I thought would just happen the right way and I would not have to spend much time or energy dealing with them. But some of those things did not go smoothly, at least not without a great deal of effort on our part — and at a time when we were least able emotionally and financially to do battle. Fortunately, many things did fall into their proper place. Through it all, we met a great many nice people, several wonderful people, and we were fortunate to even meet a few real saints. But we also ran into some not-so-nice people — people who were uncaring, some were even cruel, and some people were ... just plain jerks.

I did not ever feel that I "had" to care for Helen. I did not ever feel that I was "trapped." I wanted to care for her. I was defi-nitely upset at times, even furious, at some aspects of the health care, legal, and insurance systems. But never with Helen. I did not ever feel that the situation was in any way Helen's fault, and I to this day do not have any regrets for having spent time caring for her.

There were times when my emotions would swing wildly — sor-row, disillusionment, depression, anger, joy, rejoicing, forgiveness. I was reacting to a situation that was very stressful, and over which I often had very little control. I was upset that others out there did not share my sense of urgency in getting things resolved quickly and in the right way. Figuring out how to find a path over the moss-covered rocks was very difficult and at times very time-consuming for me.

I have a few suggestions for others faced with a similar situation. Keep telling yourself that it is doable. You need to be tenacious. Keep the faith — you need some belief system to hold onto, as it is at times a very wild ride. Try to relax at times. Know that you are doing some good ... you are making things better than they would have been without you. You are making a positive difference, and at times you will make a very big difference to the life of someone you love. All things considered, that is not at all a bad way to spend your time!

If Ray and Karyn had not been willing to take care of me, I would have probably ended up in a skilled nursing care facility. My mother had been in one for a short time after her surgeries, so I know what that could have been like. I remember the distressing smells that always greeted me as I walked down the hall to see Mom. People would be sitting slumped in their wheelchairs, or groans would be coming from rooms. I often had to question the staff about her care, and it was a major deal if I wanted to get her up into a wheelchair so we could get out of her dark room. I would try to find a location where we could look outside or even go out into a courtyard for fresh air.

While I know these facilities are needed and help a lot of people, I also know I would not have gotten the attention or loving care that Ray and Karyn provided. Facilities cannot provide one caregiver per patient given financial constraints. Further, I know I would not have been able to look at the flowers just outside my window or eat when I wanted to. Sox, our cat, would not have been able to join me. And the list of freedoms and comforts I had at home that would not be present in a facility goes on. I can only imagine the effects on my recovery process if I had been in a facility.

I am not sure why I deserved to receive such love and devotion, but I know how lucky I was and am. Ray and Karyn deserve all the accolades and love I can ever give them. I truly believe that good can come out of suffering, and the immediate good was the outpouring of love demonstrated through the actions of my family. Our family grew closer and stronger.

5

Rehabilitation

"That which does not kill me makes me stronger."

Friedrich Nietzsche

Once I had attained a reasonable amount of range of motion in my knee and had regained some stamina, I was told that I must now go to an outpatient rehabilitation facility. Insurance companies do not like to pay for in-home care as it is much more expensive. It fell on Ray to find out what facilities in our nearby community of Oregon City (about 8 miles from home) would take our insurance. There was not a great deal of choice but we decided I would go to the local hospital, Willamette Falls Hospital.

While I had never been to a rehabilitation facility before, I must admit I did not expect that the main entrance would be down a half flight of quite steep concrete stairs. That's what faced me when I went to my first appointment, so Ray went to find out how one was supposed to get a wheelchair into the facility. Surely someone else had come for physical therapy in a wheelchair! And there was a way, although not an obvious one, or even a very direct one.

We made our way past a loading dock and found doors that were on the ground floor. Then we wended our way through the halls and ended up in the physical therapy department, albeit not at the main entrance. In a way, this was another experience that underlined the lack of understanding of, and sensitivity to, people with disabilities. It seemed like I was being told over and over again how un-normal I now was. It was not something I needed to be reminded of so often.

As Ray wheeled me into the room I stared at all the equipment, which was crammed into a rather small area. It was not a warm inviting space. I wondered what types of physical workouts awaited me and if I was up to them. My physical therapist, Peggy, greeted us with a very friendly smile. She picked up where the home care physical therapist had left off and worked on my knee's range of motion, but with a softer touch. She had many words of encouragement as we worked together. She was not only reassuring as I tried to do everything she wanted me to, but also very capable.

One day Peggy thought I should try the stationary bike. I got on the bike all ready to go and started pedaling like I thought I was Lance Armstrong. Well, that was until my right leg had to go a full circle. The pain was almost unbearable and I felt like my leg was going to break. I stopped immediately as I let out a shriek expressing my distress. Peggy was very apologetic and said the bike would have to wait a little while longer. No kidding! My knee's range of motion still needed to increase many degrees before I would try the bike again.

After a few more sessions, and after consulting my orthopedic surgeon's updates, Peggy said that I was ready to try putting weight on my "bad" leg. It is rather hard to describe the fright that this sent through my system. I just did not know if I could put that foot down after all this time. It was still in a walking boot, and I knew that my leg muscles had atrophied. I just did not know if I believed that I was strong enough. I lacked confidence big time. But I wanted more than anything to walk again on my own and I did have confidence in Peggy's support and ability.

Fortunately, they had bars to support me so that I could put as little or as much weight on the foot as "I would," as opposed to as "I could." It was quite the day when I took the first few steps, even if I did use those bars to keep some (okay, most) of my weight off the foot. Peggy kept encouraging me and not letting me get discouraged. I kept trying and trying, putting more weight on my foot, and less on the bars, every session. My confidence and strength slowly returned.

My knee's range of motion also kept increasing slowly but surely and Peggy started work on my ankle's range of motion. I could always look forward to the ultrasound at the end of our work sessions on my foot. Boy did that massage feel good. And then the ice down at the end. Funny how ice continued to be my friend. After each session I was exhausted and needed more ice when I got home.

I slowly graduated to crutches, being instructed to use the adage: "The bad foot goes to Hell first and the good foot goes to Heaven first." Let me translate. When going down stairs, you lead with your injured (bad) foot after putting the crutches down on the stairs. When going up stairs, you lead with your healthy (good) foot and then you move the crutches. I would put my good foot on the up stair and then bring my crutches and bad foot up together. One gets a kind of rhythm going whether one is going up or down. Initially, since I had never used crutches, it really helped to get the rhythm going by using this simple memory aid. After a while, it became a natural movement and one I did without having to think about the adage. I had also always thought that crutches rested on your underarms, but they do not, or at least, they should not. The importance of getting the right length of crutch to match your height also became clear. You do not want the top of the crutch rubbing/pressuring your underarms. The whole action is in your hands, the strength of your arms and chest, and your balance. Those arm exercises that the home care physical therapist had made me do with weights really made a difference here. I take back my unkind words describing her.

Crutches gave me a lot more freedom. I could negotiate a couple of stairs when I was out and about, but my distance was very limited by my stamina. But I could get to

our deck on a nice day and enjoy the beauty of our surroundings and the freshness of the air.

I became quite the skilled user of a variety of assist
equipment. I used the wheelchair if I was going to be
going any distance which required no skill on my part,
just a willing pusher. I used the walker for most short
indoor trips and the crutches for negotiating stairs and
getting around for short distances, especially outside the
house. It is really a shame that walkers do not do stairs,
as they give you the most support when you are on your
feet, or even when it is just your one foot. Later I would
graduate to a cane, but that would not be possible until I
had additional surgery.

It turns out that the reason doctors in the hospital had
been avoiding answering my question about when I would
be able to walk is that they really were not sure if or when
that would happen. I had lost 2 ½ inches from my heel,
and several bones in the foot had been crushed along
with the ankle being broken. My orthopedic doctor, Dr.
Duwelius, who had repaired my hip and knee, talked to
me about this once the hip and knee had healed. He said
there was only one doctor in Portland that he thought
could help me, and fortunately he was in the same hospital at the time.

Dr. Woll was that doctor, and he had studied for many
years under an ankle specialist in Seattle before coming
to Portland. When Dr. Woll entered the room, he was all

business. A man of average height and dressed in a button-down shirt and nice slacks under his white doctor's coat, I was quickly to learn he was a man of few words, soft-spoken, and right to the point. He warned me that I might be able to walk better after surgery, but there were no guarantees since the damage was substantial. The surgery would require him to take bone from my hip to rebuild the crushed heel. He would also have to reattach muscles in the foot and fuse the ankle. I would have limited motion in the ankle, and I would be limited to about twenty minutes of walking at one time. He thought it likely that I would not walk unassisted, meaning I would need to use a cane. I figured he was entitled to his opinion, but I had my own ideas.

When I first got a full look at my foot, I cried. I was at home; doctors had removed the cast and replaced it with a knee-to-foot brace/boot. Ray took the brace off when I was going to get a bath. My foot had no heel. It just never got through to me that I really had lost 2 ½ inches off my heel. There was no arch. The ankle was all swollen and there was a long scar on the inside of my ankle where I had been deeply cut by something in the car. It was really the first time I cried during this entire period of rehabilitation. Somehow I had no idea how badly it had been injured.

It was so discouraging to think that after all the work so far, my foot still had to be dealt with. It may have been a blessing that I had not seen the foot for so long because I had never considered that it was in such a broken state. I had even been able to walk some after my first four or five months of physical therapy when wearing a brace that went up to my knee. I also tried to walk without the brace. That required having the sole of my right shoe built up so my right leg was the same length as the left. Ray had taken my right shoe to a shoe repair person and had the adjustment made. When I first saw the shoe with its two and a half inch lift on the bottom, I was so surprised. I just did not consider that my foot had been that demolished. I just could not imagine that I had lost that much of my heel.

Both approaches to walking just did not feel right. I limped badly and could walk only very short distances. Even so, I had to really think hard about going back into the hospital for another surgery. Was it really going to be better? I knew I would have to start all over with my foot rehab and that would mean more pain, more energy, and of course, more ice. In the end, the hope of being able to walk further and more naturally won out and I was back in the hospital about six months after C-Day.

My surgery was done at the same trauma hospital I had been flown to the day of the crash (Oregon Health Sciences University) because that is where Dr. Woll still worked. This time I saw the operating room and participated more fully in the process of getting ready for "going under the knife." The night before the surgery, the anesthesiologist called me at home and wanted me to decide how I wanted to be "put out." I really did not know how to make this decision as I had no memory of what had worked well on my initial emergency surgeries. I went with her recommendations. For the surgery, I had a lot of confidence in Dr. Woll so while I was worried, I felt confident that I would wake up and be fine. I also prayed to God and asked that He be with Dr. Woll as well as be with my family. As I had throughout my recovery, I thanked God for His healing touch and His continued loving presence in my life. It also helped to know that friends and family were praying for us.

After the surgery, there I was again in a hospital gown with my family looking at what must have been a rather pitiful sight. This time I had a memorable and bad reaction to the anesthesia. In fact, my whole family remembers it as they were all there to see me barf. I treated it like just another event – my dignity had been pretty well beaten down by this point anyway. I also did not want my family to worry any more than they were already. I also got a horrendous headache, which the nurse finally gave me a pill for sometime in the night.

I was out of the hospital in two days. It was a piece of cake to show the nurse that I could use the walker to get around, including using the bathroom. My lungs were not an issue this time around, nor were all the previous injuries, so I passed my ready-to-go-home test with flying colors. This time I knew I was truly ready to go home!

So, it was back to my well-known routine. This time I knew what to expect, and I was well prepared. I had all the assist equipment and I was working on exercises in the bed after about a week. Of course, my leg was elevated and the ankle periodically iced so the pain was manageable. The incision healed beautifully. In fact, I had to look hard to see the scar. It ran the full length of my foot but way over on the right edge. There was this odd short scar on my leg about four inches up from my ankle. When I asked Dr. Woll about it, he explained that he had to essentially "jack up" the bones in my lower leg so he could properly insert my extracted hip bone into the heel area. The foot did not look exactly right — there were areas where the skin and/or tissue got bunched together — but it sure looked better than my last viewing of it. Now the important thing was whether I would be able to walk better.

Then it was back to the hospital near home for more rehab sessions. Even with the heavy boot on my right lower leg, I was able to regain my capable use of the walker and crutches in very little time. In fact, when Ray asked me if I thought I was up to going camping for just two days with his longtime friend Rick and his new wife Kim, I said sure. Now this is where my positive thinking was working on overdrive. At least I didn't say no problem. We went to Cape Lookout, our favorite state park on the Oregon coast. Recognizing that I could not go far on crutches, we got a camping site next to one of the bathrooms. Then came the challenges. The step going up into our tent trailer was awfully narrow and small. I was fearful of falling every time I had to go in or out of the trailer. There just did not seem to be enough room for my crutches and me.

And the bathroom had no stalls for people with disabilities – no assist bars, no raised toilet seat, no extra space for a booted leg and crutches – so Ray had to help me when I went. It was not a pretty sight. Fortunately, there were very few campers at the ocean in September. I could not walk the distance to the ocean on crutches, so we drove by it on the way home. Let's just say my camping days appeared to be numbered.

Later that month (September 1994), I encouraged Ray to go back to school. I think he had pretty much been worked to the limit. He never complained, but it cannot be easy to be completely responsible for another person's well-being. When Ray returned to school to resume work on his PhD, I was still in physical therapy, and so our friend Marie came and stayed with me during the days. She drove me to physical therapy, helped me with my baths, and even drove me to the beach one day so I could deliver a seminar on collaboration. I had committed to this presentation a year before. I could barely get up on the stage with my crutches and a brace that went most of the way up my leg, but I did it! She also would take me to the office when I felt compelled to try to do something billable.

I did not have her stay nights, which were really quite scary at first but I wanted to be more independent. I wanted to be in charge of my life again and be able to do some things when I wanted to, not when it was convenient for someone to help me. At first I thought I might have bitten off more than I could chew. To avoid hearing the usual noises in the house at night, I had the radio on all night. It was hard at first getting used to being alone and not thinking about how isolated our house is. The radio helped me turn off my thoughts and worries, and I actually continue this habit to this day. When Dr. Ray returned home, I got a pillow earphone so he could sleep and I could go to sleep listening to interviews and news on public radio or television. Ray gave me a fancy radio that received the television broadcast stations. I can also set the timer so that the radio goes off and I can continue sleeping without it.

Fortunately, everything went fine with Ray back at school; no falls even. I tried to be extra careful in everything I did. Taking a bath on the bench in the tub was one of my biggest challenges, but as I did it more, I got more comfortable with how to do it. Of course, I kept up with my rehab work with my physical therapist and I followed her instructions very carefully. Slowly but surely I got a little stronger.

I eventually got to the point where I could use a cane. Now, even here I had much to learn. The cane went in my left hand since I needed support for my right foot and leg. The cane went down when my right foot went down but it was in my left hand. Who would have known? What was exciting about my using the cane was that it became apparent that having the surgery was the right thing to do. It seemed like I was going to be able to walk better. It was a really big day when I said good-bye to the boot and bought a pair of regular shoes – regular for me anyway. They were extra wide low boots with soft, cushioned insoles.

Eventually we were even able to say good-bye to that hospital bed. We kept the hospital table and use it today as a reading table – sentimental reasons, I guess, since it is not a particularly attractive piece of furniture.

I was regaining control of my life. I wouldn't say things were returning to normal, but I was able to make some decisions about what I wanted to do and even when. One big decision I made, even though I was still using the cane, was that it was time to start looking for a car. This would help me get even closer to being fully independent. My decision was not very settling for my family. I could tell they were worried about my doing this, but I don't think they thought I would actually take the big step. For me there was no doubt about proceeding – it was a very exciting step.

Karyn went with me and we drove a Honda Civic and a Nissan Maxima. One weekend, I even talked Ray into going with me to drive a Toyota Camry. All met the current important safety standards I wanted: air bags, reinforced side panels, ABS brakes. The Nissan Maxima really was my choice but was hard to find in the SE model. It was totally unlike me to buy the top of the line, but I guess I was feeling like I deserved it. I went through COSTCO so there was no haggling; it was just a matter of trying to find one like I wanted. Then, I got the call just before Christmas. I tried to reach Ray at school but could not so went ahead and bought it. Did I mention being independent? I drove it to our company Christmas dinner (all three of us and our spouses) and it was so much fun to drive. It just felt great to be driving on my own and in such a wonderful car! Remarkably, I had no feelings of vulnerability or fear. I must admit that Ray was not as excited as I was, but he accepted it very well.

As I followed up with Dr. Woll, I had to tell him that I was still having quite a bit of pain and some discomfort walking. He had me get orthotics made. I went to the technician he referred me to. They took an impression of my feet in a box of soft foam. The orthotic inserts turned out great. These are soft silicone inserts that you put inside your shoes that, for me, provide a cushion for my right heel and foot. In order to keep both legs even in length an orthotic also goes in my left shoe. The surgery had restored my lost 2 ½ inches, but there was no padding on the bottom of my heel. I also had to wear slippers in the house, as it did not feel good to walk barefoot on any surface.

The orthotic inserts helped quite a bit, but one of the most noticeable problems was my "claw" toes – each toe, except for the big toe, was bent at the middle joint, which made each of them look like a claw. Even though the orthotics stopped at the ball of my foot so the toes were lower than the rest of my foot, the middle knuckles of my toes still rubbed on the top of most shoes. Not only did the claw toes make it difficult to get shoes to fit, but they were a source of almost constant pain. I should say **more** difficult to get shoes to fit, as it was already a challenge with the orthotics needing to fit into any shoe I bought. My right foot was also now quite wide at the ankle and swelled even larger by every afternoon.

Dr. Woll explained that my toes had pulled up at the middle knuckle due to the trauma to the foot. He recommended taking the middle knuckles out (as in "more surgery"). He also said that he would take out the screws in my foot at the same time since he felt they were contributing to the pain in the foot. He would also address a problem I was having with my knee. The material used to sew my knee tendon back together had formed two knots that were hard and had pushed up to just under the surface of the skin. He said it would be best to remove them since they would make it very difficult to kneel. I guess that was a package deal – three improvements with one surgery. Was I excited or what?

Consequently, I next found myself back in the hospital having the middle knuckles removed from four toes on my right foot. The big toe was okay. This surgery requires that pins be inserted into each toe to keep the toe flat after the knuckle is removed. These pins stick out of the ends of the toes and you look like you have a bionic foot of some kind. It was really quite grotesque looking and very painful initially. Painful mainly because I could not keep the painkiller down that had worked for me on the last two surgeries (Vicodin). Once I got a replacement drug, I could handle the pain just fine.

So it was back to crutches and being dependent on people driving me places and helping me. I did go to work as by this time many of my projects were back in full swing, and I felt I needed to be there to do what I could. I stayed in the office and provided support to staff. I was able to work on a project or two that could be done on the computer. My foot was propped up on boxes so I could keep the swelling down.

I was told that the healing would take about six weeks, and those six weeks went pretty fast. I think that was because I could get to the office and do some things, and then I was so tired when I got home, I just slept. There was no time to think about my foot. The removal of the stitches was more painful than the removal of the pins, but it was finally over and I felt I had all surgery now fully behind me. The toes looked a little funny but they were flat. The two bumps on my knee were gone, so once I could build up some strength and courage, I would be able to at least kneel briefly on my knee. The two screws that were causing pain in my foot were a bit of a problem for Dr. Woll. He was only able to remove one and one-half of the screws. One of the screws broke off because of being so embedded in the bone. It still shows up in X-rays but is not causing any pain. I was amazed that screws that long – about three inches – could fit in my foot.

While I could not buy really pretty shoes, at least now I could feel comfortable in shoes. I even got new orthotics that ran the full length of my shoe. I found a wonderful shoe store that sold extra wide shoes, Jay's Wide Shoes. My re-tooled ankle was wider and my foot was still swollen by early afternoon, so I needed EE shoes. New Balance seemed to give me more stability and my orthotics fit easily. I also got some shoes to wear for more dress-up occasions when I would not be on my feet for very long. While they might not contain my orthotics, they were always very well padded in the heel and low to the ground.

In many ways I was so lucky in the doctor I had. Dr. Woll listened to all of my descriptions of worries or problems with sincere concern, and he came up with solutions. He addressed some of my ongoing pain problems with a pain pill whose use he had to justify to our insurance company. Bextra really helped me, but unfortunately, it turned out to be one of those pain pills found to cause very bad side effects in some people. Consequently, it was removed from the market. I decided to avoid taking another strong painkiller that could end up causing severe side effects. I started taking six Advil a day unless the pain was worse and I needed a couple more. My level of pain tolerance increased rather significantly, and I tolerated a certain level of pain to avoid taking too many pills.

As I continued to talk to Dr. Woll about my difficulty in walking any distance and for more than ten minutes, he recommended that I get an Arizona Brace. It turned out that when he rebuilt my foot and gave me back my 2 ½ inches, my foot ended up uneven. The left side was now slightly higher than the right. As advised, I went to the orthotic technician. He took an impression of my foot and sent it to a company in Arizona to have the brace made (hence, "Arizona Brace"). Now I have this leather brace that I lace up. It looks like a white boot that comes up about five inches above my ankle bone. While it is made of very soft leather, it has metal braces inside of it that support my foot and make it level. It fits inside a wide walking shoe. New Balance shoes are still the only ones that I have found that give me the support and fit I need. My left foot uses the original orthotic so that my legs are about the same length. There is a lot of extra room in the wider left shoe but it works out okay. Of course, the brace does raise the constant inquiry by TSA agents in airports. If my explanation puzzles them or makes them suspicious, I get the wand test and off I go.

At first, I did not wear the brace as much as I do now. I used the usual excuses one might expect. "I have to wear those ugly tennis shoes." "My foot swells and the brace is uncomfortable after a while." "It doesn't go with my outfit." But now I wear it even in the house when I am doing something that requires my being on my feet for more than fifteen minutes. The brace has made a real difference in reducing pain, but it has not increased my walking time very much. It is uncomfortable to wear for more than a couple of hours as my foot swells, even when I am sitting most of the time. I also cannot wear it when I drive, as it makes it difficult to bend my foot forward. Regardless of these few shortcomings, I am very glad to have it, and I am certainly glad that we had good health insurance as the Arizona Brace cost around fifteen hundred dollars!

I continued to see Dr. Woll once a year. In addition to checking up on my foot and hip, we would also talk briefly about our families. My son Aaron, quite by coincidence, had served a surgery rotation with Dr. Woll when Aaron was studying to be a physician assistant. Of course, our main topic was my foot. Unfortunately, I continued to have a lack of energy, and that meant I had difficulty walking or standing for any substantial amounts of time. Dr. Woll explained that my lack of stamina was because of the amount of energy I needed just to walk given my damaged foot and fused ankle. The Arizona Brace cannot change that. I have tried to build my stamina up with my own exercise program, and Ray put in a path on our property for me to take short walks on.

It probably seems somewhat hard to believe for those who have never experienced these types of injuries, but even with all the surgeries, rehabilitation, and exercise, I just am not back to where I was. I now know that I will not ever be there again. My process of dealing with and accepting this realization was long and painful, but eventually led to my true transformation.

6

Trying To Work Things Out

*"You can clutch the past so tightly to your chest
that it leaves your arms
too full to embrace the present."*

Jan Glidewell

As I started to feel stronger, I felt the need to get back to work. I just did not contemplate giving up on my business. I was determined to get back to my pre-crash self. I had asked Ray to take me to the office even when the wheelchair was my main mode of getting around. I honestly thought if I sifted through the files and made phone calls to clients, I would start the ball rolling again. At that time, I didn't think that all that much had changed. I mean I knew I had a few difficulties to work around when it came to getting around, but I needed to get going again and fortunately my brain was all intact.

This whole thing about not making excuses and "just get to work" all goes back to my earlier years on the farm (doesn't everything get explained these days by our childhood environment?). I was sandwiched between two brothers: Bob is two years older and Gordon is one year younger than me. I became the stereotypical tomboy, competing at everything including football, baseball, basketball, and even strawberry and raspberry picking. I suppose one could explain this drive to compete as part of the "middle child syndrome." I wanted to achieve in anything I tried. That's how I built up my self-esteem and got noticed.

It's not that I think I am a prime example of the middle child syndrome. My parents did not really give any of us a lot of attention. There was just too much to do on the farm and to make ends meet. So I looked to others for recognition, to prove myself.

While my brothers and I worked hard by picking whatever fruit or vegetable was ready for harvesting, it did not feel like drudgery. Our work days in Oregon started at the crack of dawn, but in the afternoons when it was too warm to be picking fruit, we would head off to swim in the neighbor's pond or in a nearby river. Other days we would play basketball against the side of the barn, or if neighbor kids were available, get a game of softball going. When I started playing basketball at school, I was amazed how much easier it was to dribble a basketball on a court as opposed to just dirt. I really loved being outdoors and always had a hard time hearing my mother calling me to help with dinner. This was not just a problem for her during summer, as I was usually out shooting baskets after school as well, and often in the rain.

Annually, our family would usually take a one week vacation, and it was often spent at Long Beach, Washington.

My father did not get much paid vacation from the aluminum plant where he worked, and he also liked to go deer hunting with his brother in the fall. But even on vacation, our first task of the day was to go out and dig razor clams. The week my father chose for the beach was the week with the lowest tides, which also meant the best clam digging. Sometimes we would be up at 4:00 or 5:00 a.m. – timing was important, as you wanted to be there an hour before the tide began coming in. My father made our clam shovels and we were all good at digging our limit of 24 clams. It really didn't seem like work; in fact, it was another opportunity for competition. Bob, Gordon, and I would compete to see who could get his/her limit first. No one wanted to be helped to get his or her limit. And we all loved the clam chowder Mom would make. My dad would fry clam fritters, which my brothers still love, but for me it was all about the chowder.

The big entertainment at the beach was playing in the sand dunes. Bob, Gordon, and I could make up all sorts of games; we jumped off huge sand dunes and even played cowboys as part of a hide-and-seek type game. We went swimming in the ocean – mainly wave jumping – and we explored the stores to see if there was something of value we wanted to spend our hard-earned money on. You know, like a huge seashell which you could put to your ear and hear the ocean. Such simple pleasures. The best entertainment was walking down to the movie theater in town at night with Mom to see a couple of movies during the week. Movies always had happy endings; the bad guys were always caught. And then we always got up the next morning to go clam digging.

I was blessed to have a childhood that was filled with lots of freedom and independence. I would ride my bike two miles to my friend Sally's house and never be concerned about my safety. Part of that ride was even on a major highway, Highway 26. Sally's family had a dairy farm and she convinced me to join 4-H. Now I had to have an animal to raise, and I chose to raise a bummer lamb. A bummer lamb is one whose mother died giving birth to her offspring. I fed Angie by bottle until she was old enough to eat grass and oats. Angie won first place at the county fair one year. Angie would follow me anywhere, until she had a lamb and then her attention switched to her baby. I learned all about keeping track of what it cost to raise an animal and the work and care they need. When I was allowed to go to California to work during my summers, I sold Angie and her lamb to a full time farmer and actually made a little money.

My entrepreneurial seeds were sown at an early age. In addition to raising a lamb and picking fruits and vegetables, my brothers and I peeled cascara bark, dried it, chipped it up, and sold it to the local general store. Cascara bark is used in laxatives. Dad had us cut down every tree we peeled so we could peel as much as possible. Besides, if one did not cut the tree down, the tree would die and the rest of the available bark would go to waste. Dad said it was wrong for people to peel just the trunk, which had the thickest bark. It was always important to do things the right way, not the easiest way. We truly grew up becoming more and more independent and self-reliant. I do not think we knew how lucky we were then. Our experiences, along with the lessons we learned, shaped our values and who we became as adults.

With the emphasis on summer work and using our own money for our school clothes, I acquired a true appreciation of the value of money. I learned how to shop for bargains so I could then save the rest for other things, mainly college. That and how my family lived. We shopped food sales, bought some day old items, and almost never ate out. We grew a huge garden and canned corn, tomatoes, and green beans. We ate mainly beef and chicken (yes, sometimes our own farm animals). Venison was often on the menu if Dad's deer hunting trip was successful. Pheasant, quail, rabbit, or trout might even be the evening's main dish if Bob and Gordon were successful in their hunting or fishing efforts. We preserved a variety of fruit jams and ate all leftovers. I think beef hash has become a lost delicacy, but I am not complaining.

Hanging out with boys probably also helped develop the belief that I could do anything I wanted if I worked hard enough. I was also lucky I had a mother who did not discourage me (although I am sure she would have appreciated a little more help in the kitchen). I did agree, very reluctantly, to take Home Economics in high school at Mom's insistence. I just barely got an A-. Today my family is happy that I at least took the time to pick up three cooking specialties from Mom: making pies, potato salad, and gravy — farm cooking did not focus on healthy cooking.

With the building of my independence and self-reliance through my successful efforts at work, school, and sports, I developed a sense that I could excel at anything I wanted to do. And it is not that I didn't have disappointments or setbacks, but I just never quite saw them as anything but a chance to try harder. For example, when I was a sophomore in high school, I ran for student body vice president. I ended up in a runoff with a very nice and popular boy, and I ended up losing the runoff. In my mind I thought I had lost by only a few votes. I just needed to put out a little more effort. So the next year I ran for student body president and won. As I was working on student body business one day, I came across the actual vote tallies from the year before. I had lost by a landslide.

My father was never so sure about me. When I earned a scholarship to Stanford University in 1965, I was very excited but my dad wondered why it was necessary for me to go to college. Wouldn't I just like to get married like most high school seniors living in our area? Fortunately, I had no prospects along those lines, and going to Stanford was going to cost the same as going to a state university (thanks to Stanford's generosity) — and Mom could be very persuasive with Dad. So I was very fortunate to get a first-class education and meet my first-class husband. Dad was proud in the end.

The lesson learned from my life experiences up until C-Day was that working hard and thinking I could do what I put my mind to had always worked for me, and so it seemed that that was what I should do now. My sense of humor and optimism helped me cope. Besides, Ray needed to get back to school and we needed some income as well. So I fought my loss by denying it. I tried to do everything I did before. I told myself I could do it. I wanted to do it. If people asked how I was, I replied, "I am just fine, thank you."

I slowly but surely got the point, however, that my stamina was not what it used to be. And then there was the time Ray was wheeling me into a meeting at one of my client's sites and one of the staff people there inadvertently said, "Wow, Helen, your hair is really grey." When I got home and had a chance to look in the mirror for myself, I saw to my horror that most of my hair had indeed turned grey. That will bring your positive thinking back to reality.

I decided that the old way of doing things (i.e., me working 60+ hours per week) was not going to work. I was just not able to do it. But I still did not think about closing down my business. So, I approached a person I had hired when I was deputy director of the county's Community Action Agency and Social Services Division. Ruth had continued to be a friend, and I had always thought a lot of her skills. I thought that if I could hire her to run the Child Safety Seat Resource Center and do some of the other projects that matched her skills, it would be a tremendous help.

Ruth was not super excited at first. I can certainly understand why. Why would someone want to leave the salary, benefits, and security of a government agency to come work for a very small consulting firm that had few benefits but could offer a reasonable salary? Notice I did not say a great salary. I was hoping she would see this as an exciting opportunity to do new things. I wanted her help in expanding a new program that prevented deaths and injuries to children, the Child Safety Seat Resource Center. I also told her she would have a say in how the consulting business developed. Did I mention that I almost went into sales? Fortunately for me, she did decide to take the leap.

There were other projects that I could not keep up with as well. So I contracted with another person for one of the projects where the client was agreeable. I also hired a person part-time to help Ruth. And I hired my daughter during the summer to help any of us that needed it, mainly me.

As a consequence, I had become primarily an administrator. There were a few projects that I still took the lead on, but I found my lack of stamina a real problem. One of my typical and frequent contracts was for facilitating groups, often groups composed of independent organizations, each with their own mission. I was hired to help them, usually through a planning process, to identify and develop collaborative working arrangements. This was appealing to me, as it was always a challenge and called on my skills at seeking areas of common ground and using

humor and effective communication to reach agreeable
conclusions. It required me to be on my feet for usually 2-4 hours. While I used to find this invigorating, now
I found it exhausting and painful. My life consisted of
going to work and then going home, elevating my foot,
applying ice, and sleeping.

I did not tell anyone what I was going through, although
my immediate family knew. I felt that if I could just keep
going, everything would return to what it had been. I was
in denial. I did not want people to think I was a lesser
person. It seemed like I just did not want to admit that
anything had changed. I would not even use my disabled parking permit when I was working. But oh, how
that helped me later with being able to go places, such
as museums, graduation ceremonies, stores, libraries, etc.
However, for a very long time I felt guilty using these special parking spots. After all, I could walk, just not for any
period of time. And I felt like people would look at me
as I got out of my car and wonder what I was pulling. I
can appreciate how people who have disabilities that are
not obvious or visible must feel at times. I also know how
much being able to park close to my destination contrib-
utes to my ability to enjoy whatever I am doing away from
home. But I do not park in the van accessible spots which
are needed by those who use wheelchairs.

I am sure my energy level and concentration on business
matters were affected by what was going on with the insurance company, which meant the lawyers. The young

woman who had hit me carried the minimum insurance, $25,000. That was gone after Life Flight charges and maybe the first day or two in intensive care. She had no assets. That left my insurance. I had $250,000 in uninsured/underinsured coverage, which my auto insurance company paid with little hesitation, and I had an umbrella policy to cover any additional costs and losses plus some for economic losses, etc. That's where the lawyers had to go to bat for me, as my insurance company claimed that the umbrella policy no longer included coverage for uninsured/underinsured drivers. It turned out that the law had been changed regarding umbrella policies, but this change occurred after my umbrella policy, which contained coverage for uninsured/underinsured, had gone into effect. The time between the two events had been very close, and I was fortunate that my lawyer knew about this detail as my insurance company was not going to stand up for me. Once we got a judgment in our favor, there was a brief moment of relief for my stress. Then my lawyer informed me that we had to prove that I deserved any money. That meant more lawyer time and battles. So much for relief.

It was a crazy and uncomfortable situation to be fighting my own insurance company for benefits. Having to divert my attention and use my limited energy to deal with this fight, often without notice, made it hard to concentrate on work. It also made it difficult to maintain a positive attitude, which I needed to do my work well. I had never been involved with the legal system before, and I really was disenchanted by my experience. I saw a justice system that

I felt did not care about the facts. Lawyers do not want to take your case to trial unless you have dismembered limbs or are disfigured – something where the jury can see how damaged and deserving you are. I had plenty of scars; they just were under clothing and therefore, not visible. The lawyers thought I had a good case but they wanted to settle, get their slice, and get on with their really dramatic (read: big money) cases. The insurance company wanted to settle for as little as possible. In the meantime, the doctors and hospitals wanted to be paid. My health insurance policy would not pay until we gave them the money we received from our auto insurance. No one cared about me, my suffering, or how my life had been changed forever. It made it very hard to know what the right thing to do was; I just wanted to tell my story and get a fair settlement. Emotionally drained, I settled.

Regardless of my experience, I would hate to think what I would have done without as much uninsured/underinsured insurance as I had. This type of insurance is so important, and I carry much more now than I did then. In fact, it is rather ironic that my current auto insurance company recently removed uninsured/underinsured coverage from our umbrella policy. However, our agent informed us of this change right away as she knew how strongly I felt about this coverage. It turned out that it cost very little to increase my uninsured/underinsured coverage in the underlying automobile policy to one million dollars from $500,000. I know how crucial this coverage is to protect our financial security. There are way too many drivers on the road who are either not insured or who carry only the legally required minimum of insurance. It would have been financially devastating to us if we had had to pay the costs of my medical care, rehabilitation, and property damage.

This whole issue of insurance created some tension between Ray and me. He had always known what I was going through and wanted me to stop working and take care of myself from the beginning. He saw my disability for what it was while I continued to deny it, and we argued about how to deal with the insurance company and the lawyers. He was more upset about how I was treated by the legal system and insurance companies than even I was. I became worried that he was getting depressed, and I tried to handle as much of this insurance mess as I could. To be at odds with Ray at times just added to my stress. Remarkably, we had had few large disagreements in our marriage. It truly bothered me that Ray and I did not see my situation the same. It affected my ability to maintain focus at work, and I know it affected my mood. It felt like I wasn't doing a good job at anything.

While I was concerned about Ray getting depressed, it was me that the lawyers wanted to see a psychologist to determine if I was depressed. I really scoffed at this at the time but, after reading my journal, I can see why our lawyer thought this would be worthwhile. I really did sound depressed when I wrote down my daily activities or thoughts. Anyway, I went to this psychologist and took the depression tests. Funny thing, I could tell what answers one would give if one wanted to be diagnosed as depressed. The questions seemed so obvious. Something like, "Have you ever considered killing yourself?" or "Do you think no one likes you?" I answered the questions honestly, but I did think that one could certainly easily avoid a depression diagnosis if one wanted to. Maybe it is not so easy if you are indeed depressed. Of course, there was also a session with the psychologist where we actually talked about me and how I was feeling. I found that session much more worthwhile than the test. In the end, I was judged to be sane and not depressed. I was not even prescribed any medication for "just in case" or the occasional bad day.

Eventually, I knew I had to make a change about work. In a way, this decision was not as hard as I thought it would be. I was just too tired to do anything else. I had to try to get stronger, and things were going the wrong way. It is somewhat ironic that the "hard work leads to success" attitude that had helped me accomplish so much and to recover physically, was now keeping me from truly getting healthy and back to personal peace. I wanted to find a way to get past my lifelong focus on work defining who I was and my value to society. It was time to put my health before work.

I talked to the board of directors of the Alliance for Community Traffic Safety in Oregon who oversaw one of my major contracts with the Oregon Department of Transportation. ACTS Oregon is the organization I started that advocates for traffic safety and provides assistance to local traffic safety committees. I asked them to consider taking the Child Safety Seat Resource Center into their organization and then running it entirely on their own. This meant they would have to hire an executive director. They had been contracting for their staff services with my company, Vantage Consulting and Research Corporation. They decided they were ready for this and we made the break. I closed down Vantage Consulting and Research. The remaining clients were phased out as projects were completed, and they were all very understanding.

I was devastated and relieved at the same time. Vantage was our very own business, started from scratch by Ray. Through hard work, it had become a respected and successful consulting business. I loved the independence it provided. I could decide what projects to do and together with Ray, how the business was run. We had very reliable and talented employees. I had goals for the future. That had all changed post C-Day. I was no longer excited about high energy, or even new, projects. I did not enjoy being just an administrator, and not being the doer. It just seemed like something had to give or I was going to explode. So the decision to reduce my work to the traffic safety projects seemed the best way forward. It was a choice it seemed I had to make. And I would still be working — even if just part-time.

ACTS Oregon advertised for a part-time executive director, and I applied thinking that with a narrowed focus and time commitment, maybe I could do this. (Yes, the denial continued.) This was an organization I had started and had a real commitment to, and I hated to let it go. I still wanted to make a difference. They hired me and ACTS rented a small house in Gladstone, a small community next to Oregon City and only 25 minutes from home.

I ran ACTS Oregon for two years on a part-time basis. All of Vantage's staff transitioned over to the nonprofit. We also continued to work with many local volunteers throughout the state involved in either the Community Traffic Safety Program or the Child Safety Seat Resource Center. ACTS Oregon awarded small grants to communities to help with their traffic safety issues such as bicycle helmets, bicycle education, and speed radar guns. We distributed child safety seats to low-income families. We also organized and ran the annual Oregon Transportation Safety Conference. The staff (Ardith, Ruth, Gail, and Joan) was just wonderful to work with. I would like to think we had a very positive impact on traffic safety in Oregon. In fact, both the Oregon Transportation Safety Division and the U.S. Transportation Department presented me with plaques in appreciation for my efforts over the many years. I am proud that ACTS Oregon's good work continues to this day.

But eventually I had to come clean with myself and admit that even this was too much at this time. I was not getting stronger or healthier. I just did not feel that great, and sometimes I felt lousy. I was still mainly an administrator in charge of finances, planning, and program management. Pain was still a major part of my life. I still couldn't walk or stand for more than 15 or 20 minutes without sitting down unless I was willing to suffer the consequences. And I was getting tired of suffering the consequences.

My continued work, even part-time, impacted my personal life. I couldn't walk with Ray or the kids on the beach or go on walks of any length. Anything that involved standing in line was out. I would have to go out to the car when grocery shopping with Ray, as I just couldn't stand any longer. I used to love driving to small communities around Oregon to help with traffic safety issues, but it had become very draining and painful for me. I could not drive for more than two hours without my foot feeling like it was going to break out of my shoe. I would have to elevate and ice it after every trip.

Still, the doubts about change were there. I had always worked. I did not want to give up work – even the part-time work I was now doing. What would I do? Would people think I was a quitter? Shouldn't I be able to overcome my physical problems? Why wasn't God helping me? Or was He? I was frustrated and upset, but I knew what I had to do. I prayed and I got confirmation: it was time to quit and refocus my life. I felt at peace.

So I helped the board of directors hire a successor in 1999. I tried to get Ruth to be the next executive director, but she did not want the position at that time. I am happy to say that she became the executive director a couple of years later and is doing a terrific job.

I retired!

7

New Directions

*"Even the saddest things can become,
once we have made peace with them,
a source of wisdom and strength
for the journey that still lies ahead."*

Frederick Buechner

Now that I was in the retired category at the age of 52, I had the freedom to choose what I wanted to do with the rest of my life. I could follow some of my latent interests or some newly developing ones. I knew that whatever I chose had to fit my new energy and physical requirements (I really dislike the word "limitations.") I also wanted my new activities to mesh with my ongoing desire to contribute to this world, as trite as that may sound. I actually do believe that we all should be trying to leave our area of the world a little better than we found it. In many ways, it was a wonderful opportunity to do things I had not had time to do and that meshed with my values. It never entered my mind to do nothing. I needed a purpose to pursue to give meaning to my life.

I should mention that I had this freedom largely due to Ray's completing his PhD and getting a well-paying job in software development. And shortly before my crash, we had refinanced our home in order to help with Ray's educational expenses. He also qualified for some educational loans and taught undergraduate student classes. When we had to close the business, we sold the house we had owned and used for our business in Oregon City. That gave us some additional financial resources. And then after much legal hassle, I began receiving disability payments from a professional disability insurance policy.

Ray and I had purchased professional disability policies when we were both employed by our consulting business. We considered this protection essential since we had a family to provide for, and we knew that disability is far more likely to occur than death. We bought a policy for professionals that defined total disability as the inability to do our specific jobs/occupations. This was key to us. After all our years of education and hard work, we did not want to risk our family's financial security by having to take a minimum wage job.

When we purchased our policies in the 1980s, they were very popular and easy to find. The key to our own-occupation disability policies was that the insurance company would provide the level of benefit we chose as long as we could not do our regular jobs. It does not matter if we could do some other type of job. So, for me, it meant that if I could not continue to do my consulting and running my business, I would be eligible for the benefit. The benefit cannot exceed 80 percent of pre-disability earnings, as that provides an incentive to return to work. As one might expect, this type of insurance coverage cost much more than the policies that defined total disability as not being able to perform any job for which you are qualified.

My disability insurance policy was honored at first, then stopped when I tried to get back into my consulting, then restarted when I closed my business and retired, and then stopped because the insurance company that bought the disability insurance business from my original company decided I should not get any more benefits.

When the benefits stopped, I was tired and worn down from trying to work and from the legal battle with our umbrella insurance company. I just did not know if I deserved these benefits. I had worked for a while even if my work changed. I was mainly an administrator, not the active lead consultant on projects. I had hired other people to do much of the work. I was still denying that I was disabled, even though my orthopedic doctor had said so from the beginning. He did not think I would be able to work due to my physical limitations.

Ray and I argued over this. He thought it was crystal clear that my situation was exactly what the insurance was supposed to cover. We finally agreed that if a "good lawyer" heard my story, including my misgivings, and decided that I should receive benefits, then I would engage in yet another battle. It took a while to find a good lawyer, meaning one that had a strong reputation in own-occupation disability insurance, was ethical, and worked for a law firm that had a very good reputation in the community. We interviewed some lawyers whom I felt only wanted to give it a try so they could earn some fees. They did not ask questions that would help them understand my situation or that showed they cared about me. They seemed too eager to say I had a good case. In short, they did not instill confidence in me that they knew what they were doing. They seemed more like "ambulance chasers."

The woman lawyer I chose had outstanding experience and knowledge of own-occupation disability insurance. She wanted to hear my whole story. She asked questions to clarify my situation and she was easy to talk with. From her explanation of why she thought I should be receiving benefits, I concluded that she was very principled. She told me that it was unfortunate that some insurance companies fought the professional disability policy claims, but they simply did not want to pay out the money. The companies knew that many professionals like me were used to doing things on their own and were not used to asking for what seemed like a handout. She said that insurance companies were also really good at making any claimant feel undeserving. She could tell that I was also worn down at this point and very vulnerable. She understood that I wanted peace and calm in my life. I wanted to meditate, rest, feel better, and still do good things.

I learned from her that this type of disability policy (own-occupation) was much harder to find and expensive these days because of its better coverage. I guess it is always about money. Under this type of policy, insurance companies were more likely to have to make payments to professionals who could no longer do their specific job. I was glad my lawyer had experience with these types of policies. When she heard and understood my complete story and reviewed the doctor reports that said, in short, I should not be returning to my work, she was convinced that I should definitely be receiving the benefits under the policy. She said my case was strong.

"The case was strong" did not mean it would be an easy process. There were long — about nine months — back-and-forth discussions with the insurance company, which again were very stressful. Fortunately, I could share my frustrations with my lawyer. She really understood and was on my side. She constantly reassured me, and her confidence was always welcome. Eventually, she convinced them. The insurance company decided they did not want to go to court and decided to reinstate my benefits. I continue to receive them to this day. It is also interesting to note that there was a *60 Minutes* report on this very same insurance company just about the time my claim was finally approved. Their report was not positive since the company appeared to deny claims a high percentage of the time.

While I should not have had to get and pay a lawyer to get the insurance company to do what it had promised to do when I bought the policy, I am thankful I had the policy. I have encouraged my children to be sure they have this critical coverage, and in particular, an "own-occupation disability insurance policy."

I also want to point out that this policy, while critical to stabilizing our financial situation, in no way improved our financial situation. I would have made much more money if I could have continued working, and I loved my work. Also, since I am no longer paying into Social Security, my Social Security benefits will be much lower than they otherwise would have been. I will have to take Social Security at 65 instead of waiting until my full retirement age of 66 because that is when my disability benefits will end. It means that Ray and I must be frugal, and I must be a careful financial investor.

Fortunately, Ray and I have always lived very frugally, which again relates back to our upbringings. Both of our parents lived through the Depression and impressed on us kids the importance of saving and not being wasteful. Our expenditures are guided by a budget, and I was raised on how to shop sales and use coupons. After all, my mother did raise four children on the wages of an aluminum plant worker. And Ray's mother made my mom look like a slacker, as she even made her own soap, wine, and furniture polish.

Our parents taught us well. We seldom use any prepared foods, and we can stock up on sales as we have an extra freezer and a good-sized pantry — it seems much bigger now that our children are on their own. We eat our leftovers and we also eat very well. I must admit I have not carried on my family's hash specialty. We do like to eat out at nice restaurants occasionally, especially to celebrate a special event, but the vast majority of the time we eat at home.

Appliances are not replaced until they break down or make very loud noises. I am hoping I hear something soon out of our harvest gold refrigerator, which looks somewhat out of place among our otherwise stainless steel kitchen appliances. Clothes are not replaced until they show major signs of wear and tear. In fact, Ray still wears a shirt I gave him shortly before we were married. Fortunately, it is worn only for manual labor around our house. And I wear sweats around the house. This is actually a double positive: it cuts down on the clothing budget, and I like to wear them. I am ready to go to the gym at the drop of a hat. And thank goodness, I no longer have to cut the leg open to the knee.

So now that I had a chance to look at new directions, to find new meaning in my life, what did I do?

I started with my interest in advocating for the elderly, especially those who are living alone, in poverty, or in need of human services. This interest of mine had started back when I worked for Clackamas County Social Services in the 1980s. I was the deputy director for the Community Action Agency side of the organization, which provided services and advocacy to reduce poverty, but during our planning meetings I learned a great deal about the other side of the organization, the Area Agency on Aging. Then my mother's health started its precipitous downturn and I saw firsthand how difficult it was to understand not only what was happening to her, but how to access the appropriate services and housing as her health deteriorated. And I was more fortunate than many because I could ask my contacts at the Area Agency on Aging for assistance in finding out about resources for her.

I decided to pursue a volunteer advocacy role in the aging field. I applied for and was appointed to the Clackamas County Area Agency on Aging Advisory Council. These all-volunteer boards exist throughout the country and oversee the programs funded under the federal Older Americans Act to assist those at least sixty years of age with maintaining their health and independence in their homes and communities. I dove right into the process and headed up the advocacy effort.

In fact, I guess I dove in so well that after about a year, one of the council members who also served on the Governor's Commission on Senior Services (GCSS) wanted to know if I would be interested in being on the GCSS. I said I would be interested as long as it did not mean she would be leaving, as I thought she was doing a great job. Little did I know that those were her plans and I would soon be replacing her on the GCSS.

Now I was feeling a little better physically, and thought I would be able to handle the additional activity of the

GCSS. The governor followed the recommendation of the commission and appointed me. My duties included monthly meetings in our state capitol, Salem, Oregon, about one hour's drive from my home. These monthly meetings covered two days, one for committee meetings and one for the commission meeting. After the first year, I was chair of the legislative committee, and that meant another meeting in Salem, reviewing and writing advocacy letters on proposed legislation, and also attending and testifying at hearings.

There were also special ad hoc meetings held as I got involved in special projects on my committees. For example, I worked very hard with another member of the commission, my friend Eunice, to get the American Red Cross in Portland to put together 72-hour emergency kits that were senior-friendly. These kits are important because emergency service personnel say that in most disasters and emergencies (manmade or natural), they will reach people within 72 hours. We reviewed everything in the typical 72-hour emergency kits and found that many seniors with arthritis or general weakness would be unable to open the water and food containers, use the flashlight, drink the water, etc. The Red Cross eventually added or changed the items we recommended (scissors, straws, a push button flashlight, easier-to-chew nutritious energy bars, instructions on how to use all of the items, etc.), essentially creating a senior-friendly 72-hour emergency kit. In addition, they provided several hundred of the kits to low-income seniors. Unfortunately, the Red Cross decided not to market the senior-friendly emergency kits nation-wide, but they did make some changes in their adult kit. I still encourage people, young and old, to get an emergency kit by going online at www.redcrossstore.org.

The initial work on legislation was very exciting, and I thought it was worthwhile. We made some inroads with the legislators, but overall we were mainly able to prevent draconian cuts to budgets that would have resulted in many low-income seniors losing services. Oregon had developed a model long-term care system that was gradually being chipped away at as other special interests took the legislators' attention.

I had always thought since my days as high school student body president that I would some day run for political office. Unfortunately, as I became more involved with the political process, I saw that this dream was not going to be in the cards for me. The political process is truly like watching sausage being made, as many people have noted. When you see the politicians in action, you realize how true this simile is. I experienced the difficulty of getting a bill considered if a committee chair did not want it considered. Committee chairs do not have to give a bill a hearing even if many people want it, and even if one of the two legislative chambers has passed it. Legislators make deals with other legislators to get their bill passed. Also, I found that almost all of the legislators feel they have to follow party leadership, regardless of how they personally feel about an issue.

In addition, I observed citizens being treated rudely. As citizens were testifying before a committee, committee members would talk to the legislator next to them, or get up and even walk out of the hearing. It was hard not to conclude that the decisions were already made on how they were going to vote.

And then there is the amount of money involved in running political campaigns. I could not in good conscience use that much money just to get elected to office. I could not help but think how much good that amount of money could do if used to help people. Further, it was only logical to expect that the people or organizations who give large amounts of money to a politician would later insist on that politician's support for something they wanted, even if the politician did not think it was a good thing.

Another interest I had which I am sure is very clear from previous chapters is traffic safety. I applied for and was appointed by the governor to the State Transportation Safety Committee. This all-volunteer committee oversees the federal traffic safety funds received by Oregon from the federal Department of Transportation's National Highway Traffic Safety Administration. The committee also advocates for traffic safety legislation with the legislature and with the Oregon Department of Transportation on policy. They met once a month in Salem, and this also seemed very doable in my mind, and certainly meaningful.

A new interest — or at least one I had not had time to pursue before my crash — was working directly with at-risk children. I had read articles on the effectiveness of mentoring and decided to approach my local elementary school. I was surprised to find out that several of the teachers who had taught my two children were still there, and in fact, one was the teacher who I was told to talk with about mentoring. After reporting on what Karyn and Aaron were doing, I was asked to explain what I meant by mentoring. The school did not have any mentors but decided to let me be a mentor. I guess I was persuasive (no, not pushy).

They assigned me a sixth-grade "at-risk" girl, and I met with her twice a week for an hour. I was given freedom to do what I thought would be helpful. Mainly we would talk about what was going on in her life. I helped her with schoolwork and taught her games that utilized some skills, like math, which I thought would help her in her classes. She taught me what kids were like now, problems they face, and things they like to do. For positive reinforcement for doing so well in her classes, I took her to the children's science museum in Portland (her choice!). One day after she expressed interest in learning how to play the piano, I found a room at the school with a piano. The school was very supportive of all of my efforts, although the teacher in the room next to the "piano room" did ask that we try not to play so loud. You might imagine my surprise the day my mentoree met me with "I signed us up for the talent show." You see, I had taught her that rather ubiquitous duet "Heart and Soul" for fun, and once we had it down, she was ready for the big time. Well, I did not want to discourage her, and I really thought they would not choose us during the try-outs. What was I thinking? We were chosen and performed at the talent show. She did great! I was really proud of her, and I was ready the next year for another 6th grader.

As my activities on the various volunteer committees increased, I was having difficulty keeping up. The first major indication of a problem came when I said I would help with the Transportation Safety Plan update. When I say "helping," I usually mean I am playing a major role, and in this case I was trying to direct the process and facilitate the meetings. After the first public meeting, I was exhausted and knew things would have to give somewhere. I decided to resign from the Transportation Safety Committee. They had strong people on the committee, and I knew they would be quite able to carry on without me. Yes, I had come to realize that no one is indispensable. And I knew my health had to be a priority.

Then, as my terms on the state and county senior services advisory boards were ending, I decided not to ask for additional terms. I was getting migraine headaches every time I went to Salem for meetings. My use of Imitrex, a medication for the treatment of migraines, was way too high. I came home tired for the whole weekend after the monthly meetings, and I was feeling like my three years had accomplished very little. I wanted to concentrate on other activities right now, including writing a book and working with seniors and teenagers one-on-one. I credit my initial volunteer work with helping me to better understand myself and what I wanted to do as a volunteer.

Due to my heavy involvement on these boards, I was not mentoring and I was not able to visit my then 92-year-old friend Helen in her retirement community as often as I wanted. I had started visiting Helen after my son-in-law's grandmother died. I had visited Betty between my meetings in Salem since she resided in an assisted living facility nearby. I enjoyed visiting with her so much that when she died, I decided that I would continue to visit an elderly person. Our church's Care Committee asked that someone visit Helen in her retirement community since she was no longer coming to church. I have been visiting her ever since. She is the most alert and sharp nonagenarian I have known. We play cards and bingo together. She wins more often than me, and you know I am a little competitive. I do pick out the bingo cards, so that's where I can take some credit. We talk about sports – she watches football, basketball, and golf and knows a lot about all three. She used to play golf, and so she is subjected to my tales of golf playing woes, or occasionally, my unbelievable shot. I take her flowers as my garden allows, and I take her pie on her birthday. I send her postcards when I travel, and she knit my husband, grandson, and son-in-law matching knit hats with Oregon State University's colors. She also knit slippers for my sister. She told me what type of yarn to buy and she took it from there. She is one very special person.

It has really become apparent to me that the most mean-ingful things in life are done on the personal relationship level. The programs and policies that are developed to help people in need can provide some of the assistance people need, but people need a human touch, someone caring about them, talking to them. I did. And now I can see and feel the difference I make in visiting Helen or a student. I think and hope it means as much to them as it does to me. It does not mean that politics is not impor-tant — it is just not where I am going to be making my difference. It seems to me that both political parties have forgotten the art of compromise for the greater good and how to treat people with respect.

I realized that even after quitting work, I had still not really changed to reflect my newfound attitudes and priorities, not to mention my personal physical limitations. Maybe I just did not want to face the changes at first. I jumped into all sorts of volunteer activities I knew were important without thinking about my health. I had in a sense re-placed work with just as much volunteer work. It was time for real change, to make the transformation complete.

I think I finally realized what my post-crash journey was all about. My near fatal crash created a crisis in my life. First, all my energy had to be focused on recovering my health. By focusing on my recovery, I ignored dealing with the real change going on. I struggled to be the same as I was before C-Day. I avoided the tough question of change. I did not want to change. I had worked all my life; my work gave purpose and meaning to my life. Work fostered my values of independence and self-reliance – values I had been taught from an early age. I made incremental changes, thinking I could avoid facing a true transformation. Now I was ready to own up to who I am today. My acceptance of my external (physical) transformation only strengthened and enlightened my internal transformation. This next step would be the truly life-changing step.

8

Knowing and Doing What Matters: Faith

*"What we achieve inwardly
will change outer reality."*

Otto Rank

It became very clear that I had not taken enough time to assess what the new me wanted to do. It was almost like I needed to know who I am now. I needed to spend serious time taking inventory of my life. After I left the world of employment, I had dived into volunteering without taking the time to think about my transformation. It is somewhat ironic that the attitude and determination that helped me initially recover from my injuries – work hard and you can realize your dreams – now seemed to be preventing me from returning to good health. I seemed to have substituted volunteer work for my previous business work.

I decided that instead of fighting my physical changes and denying them, it was time to embrace them and to integrate them into the new me. It was time to "get my health back" and to "refocus my life." I would use my determination, faith, and positive attitude to figure out just what that meant. I was already enjoying introspective and prayer time, so now I asked myself and God about my life. What can I spend my time doing that is meaningful to me and helpful to others? What do I like to do now that I can also do well? What brings me peace, happiness, and better health? What is God's purpose for me?

First of all, I came to realize that I was at a point before my crash where I was living a very unbalanced life – one that was very focused on work. My children and husband were away in college. I took very little time out to just observe nature, visit with friends or family with no purpose in mind, go to an art museum, travel. It is even possible that if I had been less concerned with getting back to my office to do more work on C-Day – time is money for consultants – I would have avoided my crash.

I looked back and asked myself, would I have avoided this crash if I had simply had breakfast with the Madras police officers? In other words, if I had not been so concerned about getting more work done that day, would I have avoided this life-changing event? What I have decided is that it really doesn't matter at this point. Certainly, I would not have been at that location at that time, and the next chapters in my life would have been a lot different. But who is to say if they would have been better?

It is true that we all have to earn a living and support our families, but I would suggest that we can often make some choices in how we do that so that work is not all that we do, to the detriment of balanced and healthy lives.

Obviously, work was not going to be dominating my life any longer, but what would replace it and keep my life vital? I wanted not only to **know what matters**, but I wanted to **choose to do what matters**.

It is kind of strange that my life was so out of balance this late in life, as I thought I had always done a pretty good job balancing work with play. For example, I was my son Aaron's kindergarten room mother, although I was never good at arts and crafts. I fared much better when it came to games and refreshments. I went to Aaron's soccer games rain or shine (in Oregon it was usually rain and wind) and occasionally came close to getting a yellow foul flag for cheering too loudly. After he got too tall and gangly for soccer, Aaron, at 6'7", played basketball in high school. I was very active at these games too, and I still occasionally watch one of the tapes of his games where he dunks the ball.

Now Karyn never got her mother's sports gene. She was also quite happy she did not get her dad's height gene. She stopped at 5'10", still tall by most guidelines, but not 6'+ as she sometimes feared. I tried some sports with her, but she always preferred what might be called more typical girl activities: talking on the phone, reading, shopping, and boys. My mother was so happy, as she could teach Karyn to knit. She knit us the cutest coasters; I still have some and enjoy using them. We played duets on the piano, and when she decided to take up tennis in high school, I enjoyed the opportunity to play tennis with her — and perhaps helped her make the team.

We all went camping during the summer; took vacations to various resorts in Oregon where the kids (and Ray and I) could bike, swim, canoe, and ride horses; celebrated birthdays in a grand manner; and did pizza and movie nights. Ray and I usually spent one romantic weekend a year away from the kids. And that's the really short list. I guess it was our children who kept Ray and me on a more balanced track.

Over the years when I was consulting, I had used a little country adage to encourage people to plan and take control of their lives or their organization's mission. *If you want milk, don't put the pail in the pasture and wait for the cow to back up.* It is not a Helen Decker Liere original, but I do not know who wrote it, as I copied it down from a business newsletter I read at least 20 years ago. Maybe it is because I was raised on a farm, but I really think there is a lot of down-to-earth wisdom, as well as a little humor, there. You need to have a plan to accomplish your life mission, or your goals. I knew and believed that if I worked hard in school, I had a chance to do what I wanted to in life. I always thought that things would work out well for me. And as you now all know, up until C-Day things had worked out very well for this country tomboy. The trick is defining what success ("milk") is for you in your life, and then following through with action.

I knew that I had not lost my strong work ethic or the desire to be all I can be. I just redefined my idea of "milk" along the lines expressed by Ralph Waldo Emerson in the following poem "Success":

What is success?
To laugh often and love much;
To win the respect of intelligent persons
and the affection of children;
To earn the approval of honest critics
and endure the betrayal of false friends;
To appreciate beauty;
To find the best in others;
To give of one's self
without the slightest thought of return;
To have accomplished a task,
whether by a healthy child,
a rescued soul, a garden patch or a redeemed
social condition;
To have played and laughed with enthusiasm
and sung with exaltation;
To know that even one life has
breathed easier because you lived;
This is to have succeeded.

While I had enjoyed running a successful consulting business that helped worthwhile causes, I now had to change to activities I could do within my new capabilities. As I have described previously, this was not an easy transition for me.

Work had been a part of my life since I was nine years old. Work gave me purpose and was a major part of my identity. Fortunately, as I reevaluated how my life was changing, I have been able throughout that change to maintain a purpose in life that focuses on what I enjoy, what I do well, and what helps others. And I have learned to pace myself so that what I want to do is within my new physical makeup. I think I also have a wonderful balance in my life that brings me happiness and peace.

In short, it has become very clear what matters to me: faith, family and friends, health, and helping others. There is so much that I can do to keep my life meaningful, and now that I have figured out what matters to me, it is up to me to choose **to do** what matters.

FAITH

My faith was a very important part of my life before the crash, and it is even more so now. In fact, my faith is more personal, stronger, and more active. Consequently, it was important to me to try to understand why this life-changing event happened to me as it did. Was it God's way of punishing me? Was it part of His plan for me? I think most of us would like to be able to explain or understand why really bad things happen. We would like to think there is a reason or plan in life, and certainly, we would like our world to be a fair one.

Since my crash, my faith has become a more vital and pre-dominant part of my life. I am not sure what to attribute that to. Perhaps when one comes close to death, the truly important and meaningful things in life become clearer. Certainly I had more time to meditate and pray.

Helping to strengthen my faith has been my improved communication with God. Not only do I do more talking with God, but I take the time to be quiet and listen for His response. It may be just as recorded in Jeremiah Chapter 29, Verse 13 (NIV): "You will seek me and find me when you seek me with all your heart." I have also learned how wonderful it feels to turn problems over to Him. A recent example is how troubled I had been over my sister's de-teriorating health and how little it seemed I could do to make things better. I asked God to lift this worry from my shoulders and He did. I felt as though my internal turmoil had been quelled; I felt my mind and body relax-ing, regaining a peaceful feeling. However, I have made multiple requests for this assistance as I am somewhat of a worrier.

And I should be clear here. I do not believe that when I turn things over to God, I can then just sit back and do nothing. Yes, God will give me peace – but I trust that He will also be with me as I continue to work on the problem. He may also work through other people. God will help me deal with the challenges I face if I ask. As it is written in Psalms 55:22 (NRSV), "Cast your burden on the Lord and he will sustain you …"

I have always had a tendency to question things and to try to fit things into some sort of personal philosophy on life. I have had interesting discussions with my share of ministers. After my crash, I realized that I do not have a strong appreciation for the administrative structure of the church as an institution. Actually, not all churches are run like the Methodist church, so I guess I should be more specific. I am more concerned about the "franchised" church that is controlled in many ways by a central body. This central body, or district conference, is supported by donations from the local churches and yet, does not appear to me to be listening to their member churches. There are times when it just seems to make no sense that a minister is moved to another church when a congregation is flourishing, or a minister is allowed to stay when a congregation is struggling and people are even leaving the church. The church as an organization has to be careful not to get in the way of individuals' spiritual growth. It became very clear to me that what mattered was that the church be a community of caring people who provide support for each other's faith and help others in need. In other words, a community of people who are like Jesus' disciples, spreading love and understanding.

So to get back to one of the core questions I had to find an answer to: Was my crash and suffering God's way of punishing me? I find that hard to believe. In fact, I do not believe that God was punishing me. Not that I am perfect, but I always have tried to be a good person. I mean I was driving safely at the time of my near fatal crash. I was returning from doing a good thing – giving a workshop on the correct use of child safety seats. I was working hard to support a family in college and to keep a business success-ful and growing. I even taught adult Sunday school and was chair of the Church Administrative Council. That is not to say that I was without my own transgressions, but it seemed like I was putting out good effort.

The way I look at it is that God created this wonderful world that includes us human beings as free creatures made in the image of God. This loving God does not control every move we make, but provides us with free will and the love and belief system we need to live caring, productive, and enriching lives. However, that also means that we have the power of choice in everything we do – obviously, we can even choose to believe or not. On the day of my crash, a young woman chose to drive too fast. Her choice had consequences and one of them was life-changing for me.

So was my crash and subsequent transformation part of God's plan? Now there are some who would say that God did not let me die because He had more for me to do. Was my tragedy all part of a bigger plan? I do not believe in that level of individual planning by God. Believing that would also seem to imply that those who do not survive auto crashes or other tragic diseases and catastrophes do not do so because God did not have any more for them to do. What about a child that dies? In my view, God has big plans for everyone. The way I see it is that things happen that sadden God too.

Now there are those who might find it hard to believe in a God who lets injustice, floods, disease, and other devastatingly sad events happen. But this is where my belief just makes it clear to me that God created us to be moral and to make choices. He created the earth with rules that govern nature, and He does not interfere with those either. I do not think He routinely uses floods or hurricanes to punish people, just like He does not use auto crashes. He is available to help us come back from all of these (many of them man-made or caused) and to live good and moral lives — and that is the importance of faith. While the world is full of cruelty and devastating events, we also live in a world of beauty and goodness. I believe God wants us to be upset with injustice and to try to create a fair world, and if everyone believed and acted on their beliefs, I think it could be. It is not God's purpose to make everything fair or perfect; it is our challenge. As President John F. Kennedy said, "God's work is truly our own."

I am reminded of the story one of our church leaders once told. A terrible flood had forced people to evacuate their homes. One woman climbed up onto the roof of her house so she could be saved. A neighbor in a rowboat came by and asked her to join them to go to safety. She said, "No thank you, I am waiting for God to save me." After a while as the waters raised more, a motorboat with rescuers came by and asked her to come with them to safety. She replied, "No thank you, I am waiting for God to save me." Still later as the waters neared the top of the roof, a rescue helicopter arrived to take her to safety but she still insisted, "No, I am waiting for God to save me." As the water started flooding over the roof, she lifted her eyes and hands to the sky and cried out, "God, why haven't you saved me?" and God replied, "Who do you think sent the rowboat, the motorboat, and the helicopter?"

Viktor Frankl in *Man's Search for Meaning* writes that it was those in Nazi war camps who had meaning in their lives who survived. Further, he posits that "happiness is not a goal – it is the side effect of a meaningful life." And how does he think one finds meaning? He believes that "meaning can be found in love, work, and suffering." That is because God can be with us in all three. I have been fortunate to find meaning in my life in love, work, and suffering.

A reasonable question that I have been asked is, "Do you blame the other driver?" While I know she was responsible for the crash, and because of her lack of insurance I was also caused all sorts of legal hassles with my insurance company, I do not hold a grudge against her. It was not fair, and there is no way to explain why I was almost killed that day. It was just a random event, and that only makes it so much more important that we live our lives to the fullest, celebrating our relationships and doing what is important, because we can never know when our last breath will be drawn. I do not think we can understand all the why's in life, but it is important that we learn what we can from our experiences and get on with our lives.

A short time after the crash, the other driver did write a letter to me apologizing for the crash and explaining how she was involved in rehabilitation for a brain trauma. I did not respond because I did not want to be her friend, but that is mainly because I wanted to move on with my life. I did not want to think about the crash. I wanted to look forward, not backward. I needed all my energy to help me get my own strength and health back. It probably only helped my recovery that I never felt any ill will towards her. I just focused on my recovery. It is only now that I wonder if she needed to hear that I forgave her.

The really strange thing was that several years after the crash, my daughter was taking an aerobics class and described her instructor. The instructor had been talking about this horrible crash she had been in up on Highway 26. When Karyn told me the story, I asked a few questions and determined it was the young woman who had hit me. I must admit I felt somewhat surprised at first, maybe even angry, that she had been able to recover to the point of returning to teaching an aerobics class. But I actually am glad she was able to overcome her initial brain trauma. Her disability would not make me better or happier. I wish her well, and I only hope she has learned to drive at a safe and legal speed and to wear her safety belt. I also hope she has a balanced and meaningful life. That would mean that both of us could look back on February 3, 1994, as a life-changing date that lead to a positive transformation for our lives.

To me, life-changing has not meant that my life has been devastated or ruined, mainly because I have chosen not to let it be. And God is with me to help me make that decision, to give me strength, courage, and optimism to look to the future. His love was made manifest in all those who brought food, cared for me, encouraged me, prayed for me, and spent time with me. Not to mention all the medical personnel and physical therapists. I think He has even been supportive of my decisions for change in my life. He has helped me to see what matters and what brings meaning to my life and promotes His purposes. Otherwise, I would not feel at peace with myself and when I talk with Him. I give thanks to God every day.

Now, talking with Him is what I do during prayer, and I, for the first time, truly feel I am communicating with God. Not that I always feel I get an answer or even the outcome that I would like, but I feel His presence. One time recently I even got a fast answer. I was going to give one of two eulogies at my father-in-law's memorial service. He had been such a special person in my life, as well as in many others' lives, and I wanted gathered relatives and friends to know just how special this soft spoken man had been. I had three days notice, although there were all sorts of arrangements to help with so the time I had to spend on the eulogy was limited. I wrote and rewrote pieces of my talk here and there. I worried that I was not going to say the right things or talk about the right events in his life. I was having trouble sleeping because of this worry, so one night I got up to work on it some more and then I prayed for help. And the message that came back through this voice in my head was that what I had written was good. I felt so peaceful that I did not change a thing the next day, and I felt so ready when the memorial service came.

Now with my acceptance of my transformation, it is so important to take time to "stop and smell the roses." It may sound so trite, but I enjoy just admiring the beauty of nature. It seems so clear that all this splendor of nature is a loving God's creation. In short, my turn toward being more introspective has me appreciating the ecosystem much more often. Daily, I take the time to give thanks for my life and to feed my soul with our surrounding natural beauty. I relish the glorious varieties and colors of flowers, the pounding of the ocean surf, the beauty of the mountains from our deck on a clear day, the playfulness of the squirrels and rabbits in our yard (our dog has a different opinion about these trespassers), the chirping of birds, the baaing of sheep, the new growth on trees and plants, the inspiration of music, and of course, sunsets and sunrises (sunrises being a new experience for me since I used to love to sleep in). All are simple, everyday things, but they are such an integral part of what matters.

One of my most unusual places for personal reflection time is when I am taking a hot tub on our deck overlooking forests and mountains. You would be amazed how your mind can think as your body relaxes. The hot tub is a requirement for each morning, as it loosens up cranky joints and eases pains everywhere. I flex my foot forward at the ankle to keep the range of motion I have left in my ankle. I also flex my knuckle-less toes to stimulate blood circulation. In addition to meditation, I use this time for prayer. I know God must wonder if I could not pray at bedtime or when I am fully clothed, but I am sure He knows that all of His children are unique. (Is my glass half full or what?)

I also just sit on our deck and look and listen. We are fortunate to live in the country and with trees all around us. I have come to enjoy the quiet and spending some time by myself when I can be calm and reflective. These quiet moments of reflection renew my spirit and reenergize me. I have increased my ability to see and hear what I may have taken for granted, or at least did not take the time to listen to or look for. Sometimes it is quite silent where we live. And then here comes a breeze, a rustling of leaves, a hawk floating on the air currents, an owl who-ing, a humming bird looking for our feeder, or a deer nibbling. And speaking of deer, it is truly an amazing sight to see a deer go vertical and jump a five foot fence from a standing position.

Ray and I currently attend the Methodist church in Molalla, a small farming and timber community about ten miles from where we live. There might be some who would say, "Why do you attend such a small church in a rural community when you could go to Portland and worship with more sophisticated and educated congregations?" Ray and I came from small rural communities. He came from a ranching family, and I came from a blue-collar family who lived on a farm. We feel very comfortable and welcomed in this small friendly church. In many ways, it's like getting back to our roots. And I have learned much from individuals in the adult Sunday school class I taught. As they shared their experiences, faith, and insights into life, my life was enriched and my spirit stimulated.

The most important thing is that we are receiving the spiritual support and nourishment that we need. This church is blessed with a warm woman minister who gives you something to think about in every sermon, whether you agree with it or not, and exceptional musicians who make the inspirational experience special every Sunday. While much of the congregation is older than we are, you have already read how much I respect and enjoy the mature crowd. They have such dignity, warmth and interesting history. Sundays spent with this congregation are inspirational and joyful. My faith is nourished and growing in this special place of worship.

In summary, my faith is in a God who is a loving God, and I do believe that He gave me the freedom and support to choose to make more of my life, to come back from my crash a stronger person — if one with some physical limitations — and to do good, and that is certainly what I am trying to do. I believe that is what He wants me to do, and that is what I feel at peace doing. I believe we are saved by faith but also by good works. It puzzles me how one could have faith and yet not help others.

Therefore, I believe that I have a responsibility to live by my values and to help others. In short, God's plan for me is to be a loving, learning, and giving wife, mother, grandmother, volunteer and friend. That's the type of plan talked about in Jeremiah 29:11 (NIV): " 'For I know the plans I have for you,' declares the Lord, 'plans to prosper you and not to harm you, plans to give you hope and a future.' " My disability does not keep me from having hope and a purpose; in fact, it has helped me to understand my purpose more clearly and recommitted me to it. **I think my physical loss has been my soul's gain.** I would have to say that is a pretty good trade.

9

Knowing and Doing What Matters: Family and Friends

*"Treat your family like friends
and your friends like family."*

Old Proverb

My family was so important in my recovery, and I saw anew how really wonderful they are. Ray gave up his studies to be there every day for the first seven months — until I was able to do things with less assistance. Then my friend Marie was there to help me with all the daily activities of living. She also helped me get to physical therapy after Ray went back to school and to do what I thought I had to do regarding returning to work. Our daughter Karyn helped me with some of those daily personal activities when I was so dependent on others for every basic task of daily living. And she did it even though she had a very heavy load at college. I am so proud of the fact that she got top grades through it all and served ably as her sorority's president. Our son Aaron provided mostly emotional support, writing some of the most touching notes he has ever written. And the list goes on.

It was so wonderful to have my family and friends visit during those first few months after the crash. They did not have to talk; just being there was wonderful comfort. In addition to Karyn, Aaron, and Ray, several really stand out in my mind. My brother Bob made a real effort to be at the hospital for each of my operations (except the toes, and I was not in the hospital overnight for that surgery). I felt much closer to him after that, and we see each other much more often than before C-Day. In fact, recently he had surgery, and I was glad to be able to be there for him.

My friends Irene, D'Anne, Mary K., and Ardis would come to my home and bring lunch, and we would have our usual lively discussions about what was happening in their lives, in county and state government, what we each were currently reading, and, of course, how I was doing. These friends all worked for Clackamas County at one time, and I either worked with them or for them as a consultant. We continue to have our lunches, and they are as much fun as ever. None of us looks like we have aged (yeah right). We try to talk about anything but aches and pains (we have always liked a challenge).

And then there were Ardith, Ruth, and Joan, who came to see me, and they were even at the hospital the day of the crash. As previously noted, Ardith was my office manager par excellence at the time, and Ruth and Joan were past co-workers who would later become employees of mine. They wanted to be there until Ray, Aaron, and Karyn could arrive.

Good friends who talked with me about all sorts of things only underline the importance of relationships to recovery and to healthy lives. I certainly agree with the old proverb: "Friendship is love with understanding."

I know it is hard for some people to visit friends who have undergone a major setback. Even many of the people from our church would not stay and talk when they brought meals. They would walk past me on their way to the kitchen. I was easy to avoid, as I was on the far side of the room in a bed. I imagine some just felt uncomfortable coming close and talking. Of course there were exceptions, like Pastor Gene, our friends Arlene and Bob, Margaret, Delores, and, of course, Marie, who was there a lot. Our neighbors, Art and Mary, brought a special breakfast one morning and stayed to eat and talk with us. And even though some people did not stay and talk, it was so good to know they cared enough to bring a meal. It also meant a lot to Ray!

So take it from me: it is so important to the one who is recovering from an illness or injuries to see and hear from friends and family. And if you do not want to take it from me, listen to Julius Segal, a researcher on survival, who found that "communication is the lifeline of survival." For me, it did not even matter what the topic of discussion was. Just talking about what was going on in their lives, even the weather, worked for me. Of course, it was nice that some wanted to hear about my thoughts and feelings. When an awkward moment came up (as in needing to use the commode), it was difficult for me. But one can only control certain bodily functions so long, so I would ask for a moment of privacy, and most people did not seem all that flustered about having to step into the kitchen for a moment. It seemed like I could always count on unplanned moments of more humility building.

It meant a lot to me when someone offered to do something that needed to be done. For example, one friend, Margaret, offered to clean the house and did this for several months. Not only was it wonderful that she offered to do that, but I did not hesitate to accept her help. This was new for me – the independent, self-reliant type. It is not easy to accept help when you have been brought up to take care of yourself and be independent, but I was so glad that I accepted this generous offer.

From my experience, it would seem that both the giver of help and the acceptor or receiver of help benefit. The giver feels good about her contribution to another's well-being or as I think it is better expressed by Buddha: "Before giving, the mind of the giver is happy; while giving, the mind of the giver is made peaceful; and having given, the mind of the giver is uplifted." And on the other end of this relationship, I, as the receiver, felt so grateful and blessed for the needed assistance. Further, I knew that the giver cared about me. The important thing I learned is that accepting and receiving help is as important as giving help, and in expressing my sincere gratitude for the help I received, I let the giver know how much she was valued. In addition, because I have received so much, I now feel the need to give and help others as much as I can.

There were times when I would be puzzled by peoples' perspectives on my situation. It did not help when people tried to cheer me up by turning my feelings around to put them into their positive spin. I wanted to feel like people were listening or interested in understanding my feelings. For instance, when trying to explain the humiliation felt by the way I was treated by clerks when in a store in a wheelchair, I would feel very frustrated by a response like, "Oh well, wasn't it nice to be pushed around everywhere?" It was nice to be out with Ray and out of "my special room," but it was not nice to be stared at and to be treated as a lesser person because I was in a wheelchair. I was trying to express how hurtful it was to my self-esteem to be treated so insensitively. I had lost my independence, and I wanted people to understand how difficult that was to deal with.

My experiences only reinforced how important it is to try to listen to what a person is saying and to respond directly to the feelings she is expressing. I know it is not easy for any of us to do this, but I now know how important it is. I think many people will want to look for the positive, which is fine, but it is appreciated if first they indicate that they understand what a person is trying to tell them. This is the same message Steven

Covey presented in his *Seven Habits of Highly Effective People* when he advised, "Seek first to understand." I know I always felt better when someone made the effort to listen and understand my feelings.

In fact, I wonder if there isn't a lot of truth in the old adage that posits that maybe God gave us two ears but only one mouth because He wanted us to spend twice as much time listening as talking. Or maybe it was because He knew listening was twice as hard as talking.

Another example to illustrate what I am trying to get at involves those who would tell me how lucky I was to live through my crash. I did not feel lucky for a good long time – until well after all the surgeries and learning to walk again. Often I used to think that the person who was really lucky was the driver of the car in front of me who did not get hit. I do not want to elicit any pity here, but I did lose a lot that day when I was "lucky." I ended up eventually having to close down my business, to deal with a constant amount of pain, to give up taking hikes, playing my favorite sports, taking long walks on the beach, long holiday shopping trips with my daughter, dancing more than one dance, mowing the lawn (really, I did use to like to do this), doing anything that involves walking or standing much more than twenty minutes. And when I do exceed my limit, I have a meltdown where I need to sit and do nothing except maybe drink some coffee so I can get some energy back. I cannot count the number of times I have left Ray in a store because I reached the limit and had to go back to sit in the car.

The thing is that many people just do not know this because unless I exceed the twenty- minute limit I look and act pretty normal (everything is relative). I even feel guilty sometimes parking in a handicapped parking zone because I seldom use my cane and therefore give off no visual cues to my disability other than a limp when I am tired. Those blue disabled parking permits are really wonderful, as they do allow people like me, and many people much more limited than me, to access and enjoy an event or activity away from home. When my orthopedic doctor originally mentioned my twenty- minute limit, I thought it was more of a guide, but I soon found out that he knew more than me, the "glass half full" patient.

But now I really do look at my life as being very blessed. Sure, I was not lucky that day; it was even unfair, but I have so much to be thankful for in my life. I really do believe it is important to count our blessings, not just focus on problems. I give thanks for how rich my life is in everyday blessings: a hug from my grandson, holding my granddaughter, the love of my husband and children, coffee with a friend, laughter throughout the house, family dinners. While I would change February 3, 1994 in a heartbeat if I could, my life has been re-directed in meaningful and wonderful ways. And I am excited about what today and tomorrow will bring.

Perhaps this poem by an unknown author says it best:

Count your blessings instead of your crosses;
Count your gains instead of your losses.
Count your joys instead of your woes;
Count your friends instead of your foes.
Count your smiles instead of your tears;
Count your courage instead of your fears.
Count your full years instead of your lean;
Count your kind deeds instead of your mean.
Count your health instead of your wealth;
Love your neighbor as much as yourself.

I now value every day spent with those I love. I see the importance and joy of each interaction (weddings, graduations, lunches, phone calls, etc.). I treasure my friends and family. They showed me in so many ways that I mattered to them. Their thoughts and prayers, and their actions, contributed greatly to my recovery, and they are a critical part of my life now. Ray and I get together with friends for dinner, games, and coffee; we fellowship with friends at church and we travel with good friends.

Our family celebrations are more important and meaningful than ever. In 1999, both of our children were married. These were wonderful celebrations, and I especially enjoyed helping my daughter plan her wedding. It was really special that she chose to wear my wedding dress – with a few alterations, of course. Both wedding ceremonies were held out-of-doors during Oregon's beautiful summer weather. I enjoyed writing poetic toasts for both and even facilitating a sort of Pictionary game for our son Aaron's rehearsal dinner (once a facilitator, always a facilitator?). It was wonderful to have our families come and share our happiness.

We continue to have traditions around certain holidays and birthdays. It is most unusual to miss one of these opportunities to get together and celebrate. For example, Christmas has always been a very special holiday and we celebrate not only on Christmas day, but we also schedule an outing such as a play, watching the parade of decorated boats on the Willamette River, or dinner at a special restaurant. To celebrate April birthdays, we go to the beach and rent a house. This can be quite an occasion with dogs and young children involved. The Lieres (Ray's two brothers and their families, his parents and our family) always celebrate Thanksgiving together in Greenacres, Washington (Ray's childhood home).

Our daughter has given birth to our first two grandchildren: Noah Ryan and Clara Helen. They are another vivid reminder of how precious life is. Ray and I have a play date with them once a week. I try hard to remember my physical limits. I always remember the day after all the fun when I need an extra dose of Advil. Our family gatherings are just that much more enriched by these two wonderful children, and our being able to be a part of their growth and development. Noah and Clara are also very lucky to have parents as dedicated and loving as Karyn and Ryan.

I would like to think that I had something to do with Aaron deciding to be a physician assistant. At the time of my crash, he was majoring in sports medicine. He was very interested in all that was being done for or to me and visited the hospital a lot. When he graduated, he decided to apply to physician assistant programs. This was not an easy transition from his major. He worked in hospitals to get the medical experience these programs prefer. His jobs were among the least skilled: cleaning up operating rooms and doing patient transport. But his determination paid off and he was accepted into a program, and today is a very successful and caring physician assistant. Of course, he has to put up with our family asking medical questions about all sorts of ailments so that we can decide whether we need to go to our doctor's office.

My husband and I live modestly so that we can enjoy time together as well as time with friends and family. Ray and I are not slaves to things. We choose a style of life that enhances our quality of life and promotes peace and joy. He does contract computer consulting so he has time available to travel and do things around the house. We talk more about what matters to us and spend time every evening talking about how our day went, often over a glass of wine. We are lucky to find our own interactions to be satisfying and even stimulating. Ray is very smart but also has a sense of humor, so we just plain have a good time together.

We have always been reluctant "joiners" – both having been raised on a heavy dose of independence and self-reliance. Even in college in the sixties, I was turned off by the crowd mentality that was so characteristic of "sit-ins." I often agreed with the policy change being discussed, but not with the proposed means to accomplish it. It was scary to see smart kids appear to stop thinking for themselves – and the violence that often resulted.

We made a commitment during my recovery that we would make celebrating life a priority, and we are sticking to it. Traveling is one way we fulfill that commitment. Now, traveling sometimes presents a special challenge. There can be some long walks at the airport and I, so far, have chosen not to get into a wheelchair. We allow plenty of time for rests along the way to the gates. If tours go on too long, we figure out a way to sit part of them out. Planning trips always has to take into consideration the physical challenges involved, and some destinations are no longer on the priority list. One of our most enjoyable trips that included tours was a river cruise from Amsterdam to Budapest. It was just right for us, as there was limited walking and much relaxing on the boat during which you were also seeing beautiful countryside.

Even when we choose a fairly safe destination, I am often rudely reminded of my physical limitations. For example, we were in Cabo San Lucas, Mexico, and I wanted to go kayaking with Ray out to Lover's Beach, near the Arch. Ray gave in and we took one of those large fiberglass kayaks for two out across the bay. The thing is we had not noticed until we were out in the bay that no one else was

out in a kayak, and the water seemed to be getting chop-
pier. The wind was increasing along with the clouds.
Then I told Ray that I was tired and could not paddle any
more. Well, with only one person paddling and the waves
getting bigger, it was only a matter of time before we
were knocked over by a wave. Fortunately, Ray is a very
strong swimmer and I am okay, so we swam to a nearby
beach. That beach, however, was across the bay and a
long way from the mainland beach. Consequently, we
had to somehow get the kayak back in the water with us
in it. I am not sure how Ray did it; I do know I was not
much help. He paddled us back to shore and we dragged
the kayak back to the vendor. I felt and looked like a
drowned rat. The man running the kayak rental place
seemed oblivious to the whole thing. We have not gone
kayaking since. We did later take a water taxi to Lover's
Beach. "Where there's a will, there's a way."

On one of our first trips after my recovery, we bought a
timeshare. I know that for many these have not worked
out to be a good deal, but for us it has. We either go to
our home base, which is on the Baja Peninsula in Mexico,
or we exchange a week and go other places. We have not
missed a week yet, and often we are able to also include
other family members. So while timeshares should not
be viewed as investments, if you are a planner (meaning
you will not forget to use a week), they provide a way
to take regular fun vacations to destinations you have
always wanted to see. Timeshares are also usually con-
dos with kitchens, which means that one does not have

to always pay for restaurant meals. For us, it is a more relaxing way to experience an unknown area. We probably spend more time in our room than most travelers so I can rest as needed. That is another reason timeshares work for us. We can usually get a nice one-bedroom condo with a patio or balcony that has a nice view. The one drawback we have encountered is that they are not pet-friendly, so we have to get a house/dog sitter. We miss sharing our vacations with Daisy; she is truly a member of the family.

But now we have located some nice motels on the Oregon coast, which also allow dogs, so we have adapted quite nicely. We do a little walking on the beach, but reading and listening to music and watching the ocean are my major activities. There are also a few golf courses around, so we will also play a round of nine holes if the weather is permitting (and the course rents power carts). These getaways are special times for Ray and me to enjoy our relationship without the demands on our time that exist when we are home.

I think I always knew that family and friends really matter, but now I choose to show that they matter by my actions. The thing is that I see so many people that just do not believe it, or at least do not believe it strongly enough to live by it. I hope you do not have to have a traumatic event in your life to bring the truth of this statement home to you. Time is precious and is often the most important gift we have to give to those we love. I now try to value every day and all my family and friends. In fact, I try to value all relationships. I just see more clearly now the importance of treating people as I was so fortunate to be treated and of enjoying every moment of breath I have left.

10

Knowing and Doing What Matters: Health (Physical and Mental)

"The first wealth is health."

Ralph Waldo Emerson

One of the reasons I did not feel like writing about my life-changing crash and subsequent recovery until so many years later is that I just did not feel that good. I just did not have a lot of energy. Of course, I also just did not want to think about it. I continually denied the fact that I indeed needed to pay attention to my health and disability. But eventually, as you now know, I came to realize that once I had completed all the surgeries and rehab, my health, meaning mainly my stamina and the ongoing pain, was just not improving. Work, even at part-time, was only making things worse. In short, I was not enjoying life. I decided that health matters and I acted on that belief.

I continue to see my orthopedic surgeon, Dr. Woll, on an annual basis. I am sure he so looks forward to seeing the disability insurance forms that ask the same questions year after year even though he tells them the disability is permanent. It appears that my ankle and retooled heel and foot are holding up as long as I use the Arizona Brace and do not walk more than advised. The ankle and foot will never look normal, and the ankle swells every afternoon, as well as when I am in an airplane or in the car for more than two hours. Pain has been an ongoing challenge. I continue to use 6-10 Advil a day depending on the level of pain. I still find that it helps to elevate my foot, and I even sleep with it elevated.

My difficulties with walking continue to be stamina (walking or standing for more than 15-20 minutes), and walking on uneven or sloped ground. Since my ankle is fused, my range of motion is permanently limited, both up and down and side to side. I have to be careful not to get my feet too close together, as I can easily lose my balance. Additionally, any impact activity (like too much walking) causes pain. Dr. Woll continues to remind me that all impact activities, except some walking, are out. Further, I am not to carry anything over twenty pounds.

The pain in my foot has been increasing, and at my 2008 appointment, Dr. Woll examined the X-rays and told me that there was further deterioration. He explained that the arthritis was increasing and cartilage was being worn down. He said the thing to do was to increase my anti-inflammatory pills (Advil) but that at some point, he may have to give me an injection to help with the pain. And eventually, I may need an ankle replacement. Time for positive thinking, as I cannot think of anything funny to say about that prognosis.

Then there is my hip. After the initial healing of my hip, the orthopedic doctor specializing in hips, Dr. Duwelius, had told me that it was very possible that I would need a hip replacement down the road. Well, I guess the destination is getting close. In 2006, an orthopedic doctor specializing in hips gave me one to five years for a replacement. He also advised me that I was not a candidate for a noninvasive replacement because of the plate and screws in my hip and the previous damage. The more invasive surgery is quite common now, unlike my past heel surgery, so I do not worry about it as much.

I am thinking I can tolerate the pain and it will work out that I will not need this surgery. Dr. Woll agrees I should hold out as long as I can. After all, I presently have a built-in sensor to changes in the weather, particularly cold weather.

However, I did recognize that positive thinking might just need a little help, so I decided to do something to improve my health. After gaining some improvement in walking with the Arizona Brace and after getting some rest as a result of cutting back on my volunteer work, I took the big plunge and went to a gym. I wanted to see if it was possible for a personal trainer to develop an exercise program that I could do. By that I mean one that would accommodate my limitations and not injure me further. Also, I hoped it would be one that would build upper body strength, increase my stamina and help me control weight.

It was time to recognize the value of exercise and to "just do it." It was hard for me. I had so enjoyed competitive sports, and exercising did not look like as much fun. But I have read so many articles that present studies that show that exercise can help with so many ailments and diseases, build muscles, and control weight, that it made my excuses sound lame. Evidently doctors feel that exercise can also have a very positive impact on the brain – helping memory and the thinking process. Vigorous exercise even releases endorphins in the brain and makes us feel good physically. I told myself all those studies and experts couldn't be wrong. It was time to see if exercise would help me.

That doesn't mean that it was easy to commit to an exercise program. When I had been told by Dr. Woll that my sports activities were probably going to be limited to stationary bikes and swimming/water aerobics, I was very disappointed. I had always been athletic and enjoyed participating in competitive sports like basketball, tennis, racquetball, softball, and volleyball.

In the sixties there were few opportunities for competitive team sports for women. After two years of competitive team sports in the seventh and eighth grades, there was no competitive women's sports program in high school. My high school volleyball coach had encouraged me to consider the Olympics as a goal when I got to college.

My college years were pre-Title IX, a federal law which required universities that receive federal funds to give women equal opportunity to participate in athletic programs. That means competitive teams and money for scholarships these days. I did play basketball on the Stanford women's team. This was before the PAC 10 included women's teams. We just played local colleges, and there were no uniforms or cheering crowds. The rules back then only allowed one player to play the full court (the "rover" for you older ladies). I got to play the rover position, which was great exercise, and I got to shoot baskets. As if this wasn't enough basketball, I also led my dorm to the intramural basketball championship.

To my great surprise, evidently someone was keeping track of these activities. I received a letter from Stanford many years later notifying me that I was now in the university's athletic club. I am assuming that this was not just so I could be asked to donate to the athletic program. These days I am just so happy that athletic women can compete and receive scholarships.

Since I had convinced myself that exercise was now going to be a priority, I looked for a gym near home. The one I chose specializes in Nautilus equipment. I was pleased when the personal trainer at the gym was able to work out an exercise program for me. Just to make sure I was not going to cause myself any further physical problems by following this program, I talked to my orthopedic surgeon about the plan. He reviewed the descriptions of the machines and how I would be exercising which parts of my body, and he pronounced it a very good plan. He went so far as to say that my future would be much better if I could stick with the exercise plan.

My commitment to exercise has become very strong, and I continue to choose to follow through on that commitment. With all impact sports off my list, what matters is that I have adopted an exercise program and my health is improving. Yes, I found those studies and experts were right about the positive benefits of exercise. If I am to continue walking, even at the limited amount I do now, I know I must keep the exercise up and my weight down. I might also be able to avoid or at least postpone any future ankle or hip replacements.

Here is the routine I follow three times a week at the gym. After a seven-minute warm-up on the recumbent bike, I work out on about ten Nautilus machines to build upper, middle, and lower body strength. I also use a big ball to help with deep knee bends. I can tell that by using these machines and ball, I am strengthening my arms, legs, back, and abdominal muscles. Since that's pretty much all there is to me, I consider my workout program as thorough as it can get. I also know it's about all I can handle, but I have increased a few weights and am now concentrating on increasing repetitions.

The membership in the gym is quite reasonable and subsidized by our health insurance company. Ray is trying to strengthen his back. It is really good that Ray sees the benefit of exercise as well, because it is not all that unusual for one of us to say, "I really do not feel like working out today." We try to keep to a set time like each Monday, Wednesday, and Friday at 2:00 p.m. The gym is usually quite empty at that time and neither of us is as creative in the afternoon, so it is a good time for us to exercise. The gym is only about eight miles from our house, and we can do any grocery shopping or run other errands after our workout.

Now I must admit I do not use the gym time for anything other than my workout. By this I mean many people see this time as social time, and I am sure this is probably very helpful for them. They spend much more time than I do in the gym to complete their workout because it is interspersed with periods of conversation and storytelling. They get needed exercise and equally needed social interaction all in one. I treat my workout time as serious business, something I have to do but do not necessarily enjoy doing. It is somewhat boring, but I always feel better when I am done. I want the payoff, and so I do the work as efficiently as possible so I can get on to more enjoyable activities. I do manage to harass Ray once in a while as he is working out with me, but in general I do not look on the outing as fun.

Then, to add the mandatory aerobic workout to my strength-building workout in the gym, I ride a recumbent bike at home. I ride this stationary bike for thirty to forty minutes every morning after one big cup of coffee (some days, two cups). We purchased a used bike for $150, so it is a very affordable piece of equipment for the home. It certainly increases my chance of doing aerobic exercise every day. I have been pretty consistent at using the bike, as I can watch business shows as I ride it. It's really a win-win: I am up to date on the stock market and other national and international news, and I get my aerobic workout. On the weekends, I watch a good game; football, basketball, and golf are my favorites. My business and sports interests keep the bike riding from becoming boring.

In addition, following each morning's bike ride, I walk for ten to fifteen minutes with Ray and Daisy, our endearing lemon beagle, on the path Ray constructed for me out of bark chips. It is a peaceful and enjoyable way to start the day. On clear days I can see Mt. Hood, Mt. Adams, or Mt. St. Helens at different spots along the path, and I am inspired by the beauty of each season. I concur heartily with John Muir's observation: "In every walk with nature one receives far more than he seeks."

It is fun to remember the times our family spent over the years moving plants and trees or planting new ones. Just as dramatic as my personal transformation has been the transformation of our home and accompanying acreage. When we purchased our house in 1977, we knew it was a rather dumpy-looking ranch-style house, the weeds were encroaching everywhere, and the pastures were full of rocks and tansy (a weed that is poisonous to livestock and other animals). There were relatively few trees. But the view and the privacy helped us see what could be. Now, the rocks are all in two berms with squirrels and moss beautifying them, and the pastures are mowed and full of a wide variety of trees. I think we have planted our last trees just this year. Flower gardens are large and flourishing. Our lawn adds a big beautiful stretch of green for the finishing touch.

We even survived two major remodels through the years and added a real barn. It is not surprising that we are not even considering downsizing at this point. One would not believe how much stuff we have accumulated. It goes back to our parents' teaching us not to throw things away that were still useable. Can I blame everything on our parents or what? Every time I talk to Ray about giving something away or even throwing it away, he comes up with a use for it. His office is also in the barn and people wonder why he spends so much time up there, but that's where the computers are. I have no doubt that one day he will create some wonderfully innovative software.

I supplement my workout regimen with golf. I play nine holes of golf, and the use of a power cart not only makes that possible, but very enjoyable. Ray and I do not play regularly, but we play about as much as we are able, around five times a year, including rounds with family and friends. I am a fair weather golfer, so in Oregon that means summer and early fall. We usually go to a nine-hole public course near us. In fact, Ranch Hills Golf Course is the only golf course with a covered bridge west of the Mississippi (you can see how important history is to those of us who live near the "End of the Oregon Trail"). It is in a lovely setting in a valley with a stream flowing through the course (which sucks in balls with no regard for a person's fragile emotional state).

I get frustrated with this sport because of the lack of consistency in my golf game, but I try to remind myself that I can enjoy the outdoors without being a competitive golfer (I can, can't I?). I usually tire by the sixth hole, but I continue to hope that my stamina will improve as I pursue my exercise routine. And there is usually happy hour afterwards where we dissect our games and then move on to solving the world's problems.

After a recent series of frustrating outings on the golf course, I broke down and went to get a lesson. My tee shots have always been my real strength, but my iron shots were just pitiful. I just did not feel comfortable when using any of my irons and therefore had no confidence in those strokes. I was fortunate to go to a woman whose mother also has a fused ankle and loves to play golf. She was able to help me with a new stance that takes into account that I cannot naturally turn my right ankle. This new stance, while initially very awkward, not only helps my back and foot, but also improved my iron shots. Now that was money well spent!

Family barbeques in the summer are preceded by a mandatory round of croquet. A chair is available when I need to rest, although croquet is not an aerobic activity. My family and friends will vouch for the fact that I still have the competitive spirit, although they may also say, incorrectly, that I show no mercy.

I will admit that I have often been concerned that I am keeping family members from doing what they would like to do. I encourage them to take the long walk on the beach while I rest or read. While I wait, I can enjoy just looking at and listening to the surrounding magic and beauty in nature. I encourage family members to play a full 18 holes of golf after I play 9 with them. My brothers and I have an annual golf tourney, which they are good enough to limit to 9 holes. They know that I still have the competitive spirit, just in more limited time frames. My daughter has shifted her shopping trips with me to shorter ones, and I can only hope that she truly means it when she says she prefers the shorter trips. My kids help more than ever at family get-togethers and even host many of them. I know I probably carry my granddaughter for too long at one time, and play a little too actively with my grandson, but I am willing to pay the price.

I have one area I could definitely improve in when it comes to exercise. That is exercising when we go on vacation. Most of the places we stay now have small gyms, and since all I really need is to get at least a thirty-minute workout, I should go and ride a recumbent bike. I mean, using the excuse "I'm on vacation" to avoid the gym only leads to gaining a couple of pounds that I then have to work to take off when I get home. I think I may have my next New Year's resolution.

Related to exercise, in the sense that it saps my energy, is housecleaning. I insist on doing the house cleaning so that I can keep that expense out of our monthly budget. I have figured out that it works best if I do one or two tasks a day. I try to keep to a 15-20 minute block of time, and if I am going to be slightly over that then I wear my brace. I also have increased my tolerance for some dirt. I mean, with my cleaning schedule, you know there are always going to be some areas of the house that are not ready for the white glove test. To be perfectly clear, it is not that I enjoy cleaning the house, or even that I get a great deal of exercise from it, but I hate paying someone else to do it.

I have really started enjoying gardening. It is good exercise and it feeds the soul. It is one of those activities one can do for a while and then sit and re-energize before continuing. I have a little bench wagon I can sit on when doing some of the weeding, which prolongs my commune with the flowers. There is really a sense of accomplishment to see an area of flowers blooming without any stickers or other weeds (ahh, simple pleasures). And even more than the "weed less" flower beds, I enjoy the variety of colors throughout the spring, summer, and fall. They are glorious. In spring, we have violets, yellow daffodils, white and purple Lenten roses, pink, red, and lavender rhododendrons, and lavender and white lilacs. In the summer we see the red and yellow day lilies; the white, yellow, and orange daisies; pink cone flowers, and many more. Come fall we enjoy the blue and purple asters, the red dahlias, the red and yellow mums, and the many shades of red and yellow leaves on a wide variety of maples, oaks, birch, and dawn redwoods. One can surely see why an appreciation of nature's wonders comes so easily to me. I say easily, but actually it is just recently that the beauty and wonder of these living inhabitants of nature have become so evident and remarkable to me. I am not surprised when I read that studies have shown that people heal faster when therapy includes gardens.

I credit my exercise program with much of my current good health. It has even helped my golf game (most days), my stamina, and my weight control efforts. My croquet game remains exceptional. My primary care doctor also feels my exercise regimen has helped with my high blood pressure. Recently he informed me that current wisdom is that one should try to exercise one hour per day. Actually, he left out "try." Evidently, these are new federal health guidelines. I do an hour on the three days of the week that include a visit to the gym. Other days I am pretty close. I will add minutes on the stationary bike as I can and add another fifteen minute walk as I can. My endorphins should really be flying.

You know the article that really got my attention when it comes to the value of exercise was one by Sherwin B.

Nuland in *The Best American Science Writing of 2004* (not a book I would normally have on my "to read" list, but Ray knew I was writing about my experience with exercise and gave it to me). In his article "How to Grow Old," Mr. Nuland reports on efforts to try to figure out how our declines in health at the end of our lives can be shortened. The idea is to see what can keep the quality of our lives as high as possible before the final decline, and to have that final decline be as short as possible. In other words, "Who wants to be in a nursing home for any length of time?" What gerontologists have discovered is that physical frailty and not disease are the main factors in determining whether we can continue to function independently and with a good quality of life. Two of the main factors that contribute to our vitality are muscle strength and bone density. Every senior I know wants to live independently as long as possible.

It seems to me that it boils down to *exercise or else*. I know I am convinced by my own experience. I feel better and my weight is under control (although I am trying to get it under control at a lower level).

To me exercising the brain is as important as exercising the body. Knowledge, new ideas, new skills, new hobbies: these are the stuff of personal growth. I cannot imagine really being healthy if one ignores either the body or the brain.

I have always enjoyed learning. Initially, when I was young, it seemed like the way to be successful. I always had big dreams, although I am not sure where they came from. I just knew I wanted to do something important. I also knew my strength was not in good looks, so if I wanted to be noticed, it had to be in academics or athletics.

Good grades in high school came easy, and I was fortunate that Stanford University took a chance on me. Can you imagine my surprise when I got there and everyone was a valedictorian, or a student body president? My learning started immediately, even before classes. Most of the students were much more sophisticated than I was. I would watch during meals so I would learn how to handle multiple forks and spoons at dinner, not to mention multiple plates. I had never had some of the dishes that were served such as lamb with mint jelly, chicken cacciatore, baked Alaska, lasagna, and many more. I mean on the Decker farm, we were into meat and potatoes.

Of course, the classes were even more wonderful than the meals and quite challenging. I give Stanford credit for getting me to think critically and to evaluate and truly learn. I became interested in ideas and applying knowledge. It became clear that learning wasn't "just the facts, ma'am, just the facts." Or perhaps Confucius puts it a little more eloquently: "Learning without thought is labor lost."

I have been learning ever since. One might call it exercise for the brain. I know that learning is something that matters just as much in my retirement years. Our minds are what make us humans so special, and we should not only value them, but continue to use them and expand them. I feel that my mental health depends on it. Learning makes life so much more special. I was always learning in my job as consultant to nonprofits and government agencies. There were new programs to write grants for, or for me to develop. I learned to like public speaking and to do it pretty well. I learned all about managing nonprofits and how to run a business.

Now, without work, there are still many ways for me to continue my learning. This is one place where my physical limitations are not a major concern. I have so many interests that I now have time to pursue. Reading is certainly one means of pursuing my interests in history and political science. I continue to read history books, with biographies being a special interest of mine. They provide such insight into how individuals have shaped our world and how human (as in having flaws) revered leaders are. My friends also make recommendations to add variety and spice to my reading experience. Their recommendations provide a break from my nonfiction addiction. I also love to give books as gifts. For Christmas, my brother Gordon often receives a copy of the history book I have recently read and given a "thumbs up" review. My nieces and mother-in-law receive my preferences in fiction.

I have enjoyed art and art history ever since taking art history in college and then seeing so many of past centuries' works of beauty and insight in Europe. Whenever we travel to a city with an art museum that I have heard or read about, I try to work in a visit. I have been fortunate to visit some awe-inspiring exhibits at museums around the world as well as right here in Portland, Oregon. I go to the art museum for lectures and can always find a place to sit and rest while touring the exhibits. The Portland Art Museum has a monthly "Art and Conversation" event. The event is free to those 55 and older unless there is a special exhibit to tour, and then it costs the price of admission. It is a wonderful time to meet new people and to learn more about the history and insight of artists of the world.

And there are other areas of learning that are practical and enjoyable. There is the area that is important to our financial stability – i.e., investments and financial management. I have learned about investing so that I can manage our finances. Obviously, this is something I can do without standing or walking, so it has been a natural fit for me. I also find investing, retirement planning, business issues, and the economy very interesting. This interest might stem from my early employment in a savings and loan, and then later having been in charge of the financials of our business. In fact, I probably listen to and watch way too many stock and investment shows on radio and television. I have always been very good with numbers and have enjoyed learning about retirement planning. I have read many excellent books and subscribe to two business magazines. Let's hope I have learned well. (I know Ray hopes so.) I feel confident that our financial plans are sound even though one must make a few assumptions. It is important that we manage our own funds, as no one cares about our retirement and financial security as much as we do. By the way, it is not that hard. Anyway, so far, so good.

And there are other areas of learning that are insightful and inspirational. For example, there has also been much to learn about classical music. While I played some classical music on the piano while growing up (not "Heart and Soul"), I did not gain a true appreciation for symphonies until much later. Ray has probably been a better teacher in this area than anyone. And I have returned the favor by dragging him to plays which are not only enjoyable but often offer insight into human relationships. And there is always much to learn of religion and faith to enrich my soul and life.

I enjoy learning through listening to public television and radio as well. Because I still have some trouble sleeping at night, I enjoy listening to the music and programs on public radio. I truly have my crash to thank for reintroducing me to the radio. When I was growing up on the farm in the fifties, my family listened to a variety of programs and sports events on the radio. That came to an end when we could afford a television. Up until C-Day, I had only listened to music stations on the radio in the car. During my recovery, daytime TV just did not have much to keep my interest, so I listened to radio programs, many of which were educational. I enjoyed it and I think it sharpened my listening and concentration skills. Later, recognizing broadcast television's programming limitations, Ray added cable for me so I could watch sports and hear more news. I have developed an appreciation for public television, as well as some cable stations, that have very informative presentations on former presidents, influential people, and important historical events.

And looking to the future, there are two more things I would like to learn to do: speak Spanish and quilt. Fortunately for us seniors, there are reduced fees in community education programs, community colleges, and even some universities. There are quilting groups, book clubs, hiking clubs, bird-watching groups, etc. Learning opportunities abound. Learning will continue to matter to, and enrich, my health and my life.

Now I know that exercise – physical and mental – is not the only activity important to living a healthy life. A person's health also depends on living a balanced life and doing all of the things that matter. In the next chapter, I conclude with taking a look at how I have balanced my life so that it is vital and meaningful.

11

Knowing and Doing What Matters: Helping Others

"I've seen and met angels wearing the disguise of ordinary people living ordinary lives."

Tracy Chapman

Helping others is something I have always had as a priority, and after my crash it only seems more important. Take it from me, I know compassion and selfless caring matter. I have received so much help, love, and support from others, and I know how critical that help was to my recovery. There are so many ways in which we can help others. It is our commandment from God to love one another. That call for us to provide compassion and caring help applies not just to family and friends, but also to strangers. As Paul wrote in his letter to the Philippians Chapter 2, Verse 4 (NIV), "Each of you should look not only to your own interests, but also to the interests of others."

I was so fortunate to have a profession where my job was to assist nonprofits and government agencies with their efforts to help disadvantaged people. One way I did that was by writing grants for organizations so that they could have the money to start innovative or new programs, like helping addicted mothers and their babies, or setting up a homeless shelter, or bringing heritage organizations together so that they could optimize their tourism and educational efforts. I helped communities throughout the state of Oregon improve traffic safety efforts and started the Child Safety Seat Resource Center. Although running my business and working on efforts like these are no longer possible for me, it does not mean that I have to stop helping others. I just need to find other ways. What matters is helping people.

I found when I was volunteering that I truly enjoy and am pretty good at visiting seniors and mentoring youth. What those two activities have in common is that they are based on one-on-one relationships. Much of that activity can be done sitting and talking, playing a game, discussing a book, doing homework, or even playing the piano.

I got my interest in visiting seniors from when I was visiting my mother as her health deteriorated. Ultimately, she had to be in an adult care home since I could not care for her in my home. I visited about every other day as I knew her time was limited. Those visits were very special, even though often I was the only one talking as she would slip into periods of unconsciousness. She had brain cancer, and when she was awake, she would sometimes tell me weird stories. One morning she told me that she had run off to Mexico and gotten married. I was told by the caregiver that I should not challenge these stories as they were harmless, and she did not need to hear that she was being irrational. My daughter would go with me sometimes, and my son went to see her in his high school graduation gown, as she was not able to leave the adult care home to attend his graduation. She was so proud of them, and the day before she died, she woke up, recognized Karyn, and talked to her like nothing was wrong.

Then when I was participating on the Governor's Commission on Senior Services in Salem, I would visit my son-in-law's grandmother between committee meetings. Betty was residing in an assisted living facility in Salem. Visits with her would always improve my day. Even though her health was failing, she always had a wonderful attitude, and I would so enjoy talking with her about her life as well as about Karyn and Ryan (her grandson). My memory of her is so special that I take flowers to her grave on my way to visit my parents' grave sites. While some people avoid cemeteries like the plague, I find the quiet a special time to remember and honor loving relationships.

I also learned of the threat that isolation and lack of social interaction poses to the mental health of elderly people while participating on the Governor's Commission on Senior Services. Isolation can lead to depression, which impacts a person's quality of life and can lead to suicide. The suicide rate among the elderly is higher than for other age groups.

By visiting elderly people, I feel like I am helping another person. I can see the impact I have. I also benefit from the friendship and enjoy hearing of the wonderful life experiences these women have had. It is time so well spent, and I come home feeling refreshed and blessed by their friendships. It seems the giver of love benefits as much as the receiver. Or as James M. Barrie put it, "Those who bring sunshine into the lives of others, cannot keep it from themselves."

What is meaningful to me now is direct contact with an individual, where I can help or just be nice to someone. And what is remarkable, maybe even ironic, is that that is what I have — and everybody has — the physical strength and ability to do. In other words, not only do I no longer have the stamina and physical ability to run my consulting business, it is also no longer where my true interest or heart is. It makes my day to visit my now 97- year-old friend in a retirement center, my 84-year-old friend living alone, play with my grandson, hold my granddaughter, help my sister, tutor a child, or have lunch with a friend. I agree with Charles Dickens when he wrote in *Our Mutual Friend*: "No one is useless in this world who lightens the burden of another."

I am not sure if my increased awareness of the importance of relationships is related to my increase in intensity of feelings or not, but that is another difference growing out of my life-changing experience. I cry more easily and laugh more readily (which is saying something since I have always had a tendency to see the humor in life). I seem to have a heightened sense of the feelings involved in caring relationships and the human condition in general. I mean, it can even be a TV show that has a touching moment that brings on a few tears. I hug people more often, although I do restrain myself from hugging strangers. I hope I am not going to get calls from psychologists. I just feel much more in touch with all of life, and I think I just appreciate it and people more.

One other activity that I discovered I enjoyed and that is also aimed at helping people is writing. I decided that I should try to do more writing, as it had come easily for me in the past. By that, I mean in my work I did a lot of writing of reports, grants, brochures, meeting summaries, and manuals. Now I can concentrate on topics that bring my life meaning and that will hopefully inspire others. My writing now is a much more personal and creative activity, not to mention, more challenging.

Now when it comes to helping others, I love to talk about my volunteer work. As mentioned before, since retiring, I have been doing volunteer work: mentoring at-risk girls, visiting elderly women, and serving on advisory boards. My writing has taken time away from time spent volunteering, but now that I have completed this book, I hope to be able to increase my volunteer efforts.

Volunteer work for those of us in retirement could also be looked upon as an essential part of our new life. In fact, Richard N. Bolles, in his book *The Three Boxes of Life*, reported that among those who had no plans for retirement, seven out of ten die within two years. I guess that's using the stick instead of the carrot approach to recruiting volunteers. But here's the carrot: research has found that older people who volunteer have better physical and mental health, and a lower mortality rate.

I certainly know how important it is to be spending part of my time doing meaningful work – to me that means helping someone. As a baby boomer, I remember President John F. Kennedy's call for civic involvement in the early 1960s, and just think how wonderful it would be if people made a lifelong commitment to help people and to improve society.

Volunteerism has been a very interesting and vital part of my life and work. I have observed it, worked with it, done it, am doing it, and have consulted on it. Here are a couple of observations I would make:

- Opportunities for volunteering are increasing as agencies depend more on volunteers in tight budget times. Volunteers can choose positions that match their skills and personalities. Many of the positions include high levels of responsibility. Examples of volunteer positions include: teaching a safe driving course for AARP, providing financial management for seniors, doing taxes for seniors, providing advice on insurance (Medicaid and Medicare), mentoring children, serving as foster grandparents, and providing medical services in clinics. One can choose to be on a policy-setting and advocacy board for a wide range of programs such as domestic violence shelters, homeless shelters, aging, and traffic safety. One can and should choose to volunteer for an agency or program that is personally meaningful.

- Volunteering is not just for the retired; it is a life-long enrichment activity and should be encouraged and supported early in life. I know many universities require or look with favor on high school students who have volunteered in their communities. I especially enjoy hearing of youth-senior collaborative projects. For example, seniors serving as lunch buddies at elementary schools or high school students helping out at nursing homes. And here's the carrot: it has been reported that teens who help others are less likely to join gangs, use drugs, or become pregnant.

- Volunteers are more educated than ever and more diverse in age, ethnicity, background, and experience. Agencies will need to continue to develop responsible volunteer positions as financial resources continue to be scarce.

- There are volunteer resource agencies in most counties that match volunteers to organizations. Check the community pages in your phone book, dial 211 for information and referral, call 1-888-826-9790, or go online at www.1-800-volunteer.org.

My intent in writing books is to be of help and inspiration to people. Hopefully, this will be my first successful effort at writing a book, and not my last. I had declined from taking new terms on the two boards involved with seniors in part because I believed I could better advocate for elders by writing a book on senior resources. My approach when I started writing the book had not been used. I searched the Internet and local bookstores to verify this. I wanted to write a comprehensive guide for the adult children of aging parents. It was apparent to me that people did not know how to access the services or to find the help their parents needed. I knew most of the resources from my advocacy work on the Governor's Commission on Senior Services and on the Clackamas County Area Agency on Aging Advisory Council, and I knew how to access them. I gathered the informational materials, wrote my table of contents, the introduction, and two chapters.

Then I wrote my book proposal to see what the response of an agent would be. I had found out that a writer no longer submits her work or book proposal directly to a publisher. For the most part, publishers have stopped reading them as they were inundated with manuscripts and proposals. They now rely on agents to do the screening for them. As I was writing my book proposal, I came to the section where I needed to present my marketing plan. As part of that plan, I was to explain why my book would be bought off the shelves of a bookstore rather than any other in the same category. I decided I needed to update my marketing research, and that is when I ran into trouble. Someone had written a book like I was writing. It had just hit the book store shelves. Not only that, but it had the endorsements of AARP, doctors, the *Ladies' Home Journal*, etc.

I bought the book to be sure it really did what I thought it did – and it did. It pretty much provides help for most of the issues and decisions faced by the elderly. In case you are in need of such a wonderful guide, *How to Care for Aging Parents* by Virginia Morris should help. Do not let the size of the book deter you; you can read the sections that apply as issues come up.

That is when I decided to write a book I knew no one else could write, and I knew this would hold the possibility of helping and inspiring others facing change and challenge in their lives. And after all, authors are supposed to write about what they know. Now that I have finished my story, I have been thinking about other subjects I would like to write about. Not surprisingly, the possible subjects are the elderly (nonfiction) and a fiction book for teenagers. I feel I could draw on my experiences with both groups, so we will see where my inspiration takes me.

Now, even though I know reaching out to others matters, I have found that I am not as successful at doing it as I would like to be. I am a work in progress, but I know from my own experience how important this type of personal outreach is. When someone says something that hurts my feelings or just strikes me as wrong, I, all too often, respond too strongly, sometimes even angrily. I feel like I have to right the wrong without first understanding what may be going on with the other person. After I realize my blunder, I feel guilty and recommit myself to sticking to my mother's constant guide, "If you can't say something nice, don't say anything." Now, I figure that doesn't mean that I cannot express my opinion or even offer constructive criticism, but first I have to try and understand just what the person is trying to say. Now, I am trying not to interrupt or finish someone's sentence. Once I understand (or at least think I do) and it is something I just cannot agree with or let pass, I am trying to offer my opinion in a way that is not hurtful or disrespectful. I know it really does make a difference when you treat people as you would want to be treated. I need to practice what I preach.

I do make a point to take time to ask clerks, gas station operators, just about anyone I run into, how they are doing and closing with "have a good day." In fact, I usually engage in a lively banter about the weather or traffic or something I think might call for a response. A "thank you" is also something that can never be overrated — as the recipe says, "add generously." It is all too easy to only focus on what we want and forget that everyone has feelings and deserves to be treated kindly and with dignity. It is a feel-good strategy, and it works for me.

I am also trying to think less about myself and more about others in other ways. I try to be the good listener and not to turn the conversation back to me. A good example of the change is the difference between my twenty-fifth and fortieth high school reunions. I had looked forward to my twenty-fifth, which was pre-crash, so I could impress people with my family and my achievements. In other words, I was thinking mainly of myself. However, the dinner dance was in a dark ballroom at the local Elks Club, and I could see few of my friends to thrust myself upon. Ray and I ate and danced once or twice before leaving early. I felt it was a total disappointment.

When my 40th reunion came, a friend called to ask why I had not signed up to attend, as she was going and had hoped to talk with me. I decided to go and had a wonderful time. I got a chance to talk with a number of friends, and learned about how well their lives had progressed. It was a perfect setting – a summer barbeque at an outdoor park on Mt. Hood (ironically, not far from my crash) – where I could see, talk with, and listen to those with whom I had grown up. I was really proud of my classmates – and it was great to hear of their experiences and to just joke around.

With my experience in a wheelchair, with a walker, with crutches, and with a cane, as well as my volunteer work as an advocate for seniors and people with disabilities, I have a new and profound respect for people with disabilities. I experienced the difficulties of access and acceptance faced by people in wheelchairs and using other assist equipment. I know in a deeply personal way some of the indignities many people with disabilities face in their daily lives. I can spot a well or poorly designed bathroom for people with disabilities in an instant. The placement of the assist bars is my hot button. I am disappointed with how steep some of the ramps are constructed for people with disabilities, and even the location of some of the parking spots. I am glad that many people have motorized chairs now.

People with disabilities just want to be treated with respect and like anyone else. It hurts to have people not look you in the eye or talk to you. I, therefore, always try to treat people with disabilities with the respect they deserve. Before I help anyone with a visible disability by holding a door, I ask if I may help them. People with disabilities are striving for independence (and boy, do I understand that) and some may not appreciate someone thinking they cannot get their own door or do whatever task you would like to help them with. Many others will appreciate the assistance and the reaching out of the hand to help.

As an advocate for seniors, I also encourage people to reach out to homebound seniors or seniors living alone. Isolation can be so detrimental to the mental health and well-being of an elderly person, and we can learn so much from the wisdom and experiences of seniors. Although I am a senior under many definitions of that term, I still feel I learn from visiting my senior friends. If you do not know how to find out about seniors who need visitors, check with your church or local senior center.

As a mentor (currently on hiatus) for young at-risk girls, I would hope more adults would reach out to those who are part of our country's future. The children who need our help are not responsible for their parents' divorces, drug or alcohol use, or unemployment. They only need our love and attention to help them focus on their development and future. I am always discouraged when I see children who have not learned to read or write by the time they are twelve years old. I found working with young girls kept me up on what was new with kids, what they were thinking, and what motivated them. I also found that they truly appreciated time spent with them, even with someone who could be their grandmother. It was a win-win for both of us.

I would like more people to join me in heeding the wisdom of the first century Rabbi Hillel, who said, "If I'm not for myself, then who will be? But if I am only for myself, then what am I?" For those of us in retirement, volunteer work could be looked upon as an essential part of our "new" life. It is so important to spend part of our time doing meaningful things, things that help others. We all need to take care of ourselves and our families, but we can also reach out and help others who need a helping hand in some way in order to grow into healthy, productive, and life-loving individuals. To me, it is an essential part of my life's mission.

When I was recently in California dealing with some very hard issues with my sister's health, my heart was so warmed by strangers who sensed my sister's difficulties and showed such caring. For example, one man helped us with self-serve gas, something as an Oregonian I had little experience with. That afternoon I was tired and frustrated with not being able to put gas in my sister's car. His help lifted a load from my shoulders. When we thanked him, he replied, "Isn't that what we are supposed to be all about, helping others?" Yes, indeed.

I have become a strong advocate for "random acts of kindness." I encourage others to experience the joy of listening to someone or thanking someone for his or her kindness. Call a friend or relative to have coffee with you. Help a child learn to read. Play bingo with an elderly friend. Attend a niece's wedding or graduation. I have found that helping or supporting someone makes me happier too. It is truly time well spent. In fact, I read recently in our local newspaper, *The Oregonian*, that the "emerging science of happiness has found that the single biggest determinant of our happiness is the quantity and quality of our relationships."

And if you think that you do not have enough time or energy to make a difference in someone's life, let me refer you to Edmund Burke:

Nobody makes a greater mistake
than he who does nothing
because he could only do a little.

༒

So let's use a chart to see how all of my activities fit into a balanced approach to life, and particularly one that has me doing the things that I say matter to me. The grant writer stirs from within. You will note that some activities really fit in more that one category. For example, my path walks are exercise but also a time I use to feed my soul by observing the wonders of nature. They are also a special time to talk with Ray about our day and therefore could also fit under my commitment to family/friends. I find that trying to fit things into discrete categories is not that clear-cut. However, I do think this exercise has been a good one for me since I want a balanced life and I want to do what matters. The chart makes it easier to see that I am doing a pretty good job of that. And I know that, for I am happy and at peace. You may want to make a chart of your life activities to see how balanced your life is.

Helping Others	*Family/Friends*
visiting seniors	grandkids
writing	family get-togethers
youth mentor	lunches/dinners
	travel
Health	*Faith*
path walks	prayer
gym	observing/reflecting
stationary bike	church
learning activities	gardening

Now there may be some who would say, "Gee, that is nice for you, Helen, but I have to work." My reply would be that I certainly agree that work is very important, essential even. I loved work; it reinforced and built my self-esteem. It was very hard for me to give up paid work. Helping others was my job. Now, however, it is volunteer work. The important thing in looking at how one spends one's time is that one has balance in her/his life. I would maintain that a balanced life is a healthy life, and such a life is not all about work, or all about learning/school, or all about exercise, etc. It is about knowing what matters to us, what and who is important in our lives, and then choosing to include those activities and people in our daily lives.

So what matters to me after my transformation? It has become so clear for me now. Now I want to balance my life with my passions: family and friends, faith, helping others, exercise, and learning. I want to spend my time with the activities, thoughts, and people that bring me peace, health, and happiness. I truly hope I can bring the people whose lives I touch love and joy. I feel so blessed to have such wonderful balance back in my life.

I encourage everyone to think about what they value in their lives. What would you want written on your gravestone or remembered about you? Are you spending your time doing what is really important to you? Do you feel like meaning is missing in your life? Have you got a balance in your life among working, spending time with family and friends, helping others, exercise, learning, and meditation?

My transformation has taught me so clearly how wonderful I feel when I am living life fully. Time is so valuable, and it is also the most important gift you have to give.

✎◗ ◖✎

There is a very practical side to getting your life in balance. Knowing and doing what matters makes it so much easier to decide whether to decline certain invitations to do something. This has been life changing for me. It has always been hard for me to say no. For example, our church organized a stewardship process that included education on all of the church committees and their work. Because I knew that I would prefer to do something to help an individual, and I am particularly concerned about the elderly, I asked our pastor if there was someone who needed regular weekly visits. She was intrigued, and a short time later, asked me if I would visit Shirley. It has turned out to be a wonderful relationship.

Shirley had a serious fall when visiting her great-granddaughter in Tennessee, and because the leg that was broken had already had a knee replacement, the healing process was a long and hard one. At the time I started visiting her, she was not able to drive, was using a walker, and really needed someone to visit her in the assisted living facility. Now, she lives independently by herself. We talk on all sorts of subjects. She is a fascinating individual with a lifetime of great experiences. We play Sequence regularly; I bring her books to read, some days we share a devotional, and we occasionally venture out for errands or lunch.

Now our pastor did ask me if I wanted to visit an additional person, but I declined because I knew it was important to me to also finish this book, spend time with my grandchildren and Ray, exercise, etc. And I felt at peace declining because I knew I needed to keep my life in balance and do all of the things that matter. I did get talked into signing up for one church committee, but it does not meet often. And I also led an adult Sunday school class, but just for eight weeks.

In summary, success to me now is enjoying my family and friends, strengthening my faith, staying healthy, learning more about history, art, and people, and contributing to society primarily through my writing and supportive relationships with the elderly and youth. It is being at peace with who I am, and I think that I am now a more caring and thoughtful person, but also one that is still learning, exercising, meditating, and helping others.

Life is wonderful even when it takes some very difficult detours. It truly makes a difference in how one chooses to react to life-changing events. My life is richer as a result of this difficult journey. My disability is not a roadblock, just a detour, a redirection. It took me a while (okay, years) to come to grips with my life's transformation, but I have now embraced it for the new riches it brings. And I am blessed to have so many loving family members and friends who have supported and accompanied me along the way.

I am at peace with who I am now. I have changed. Slowed down with ongoing pain and less energetic, but also more aware and appreciative of all I see and feel. The internal and external parts of my life are more in balance. I am thankful for my life, and I am more committed than ever to making a difference in other people's lives. I have found that when I am helping others, I am helping myself. My story is truly a transformation story in addition to being a survival story – a story of embracing the new me and seeing the new opportunities for a meaningful and happy life.

12

Decide to Change

"This is the day the Lord has made;
let us rejoice and be glad in it."

Psalms 118:24 (NIV)

One reason I wrote this book is to help those who have lost a physical ability, or may face such a loss in the near future. It was hard for me to change, but that is what I finally decided to do. I realized I was not going to be the same as I was before February 3, 1994. I decided that I was a permanently changed person and that was okay. There were still things for me to do; they were just different. I could still enjoy life, just in different ways. I could still make a difference in this world, particularly in the lives of my family, the elderly, and at-risk youth.

That sounds easy to say, but as you know from reading the previous chapters, it took a while for me to come to this realization. Also, as you have also hopefully gleaned from the previous pages, it has been a revitalizing transformation. I have been able to do things that I was not able to do previously because I had to run a business. Yes, I enjoyed my business work, for it was also aimed at helping make a difference in this world. But now I can work on making a difference in individuals' lives. And that is a difference I can see and feel. It makes my efforts more personally meaningful.

And since February 3, 1994, I have accepted, even embraced, many changes. Now, instead of taking long walks on the beach, I take a short walk and then I sit and enjoy all that is alive and wonderful around me. Instead of playing tennis, basketball, racquetball, or volleyball, I use a power cart to enjoy nine holes of golf, and I exercise on my recumbent stationary bike and on Nautilus equipment. Instead of dancing the night away, I enjoy one dance, maybe two, and then enjoy the music (this may be one of the most difficult social activities I have had to forego). Instead of mowing the lawn, I enjoy gardening from my work bench wagon. Instead of writing grants and traffic safety newsletters, conducting workshops, and facilitating groups, I volunteer with seniors and youth. Instead of rushing around each day working, I take time daily to read, take a short walk with my husband and dog, meditate, and write. It is amazing what I can do when I need to be sitting and regaining some energy. Instead of all day shopping trips, I shop in one or two stores, sitting when I need to and finishing off with lunch. Instead of making excuses about being too busy at work, I attend relatives' weddings, graduations, and other special events or help with health issues. I call up a friend for coffee just to talk and laugh or go see something new or interesting in the area.

For quite a while, I could not bear the thought of not having my business and doing the work that was so important to me. Now, I truly am reinvigorated and redirected in a life that I find much more peaceful and satisfying. I still am trying to be the best person I can be, and finding a closer relationship with God has made my life more meaningful. Not only did I survive my near fatal crash, but my transformation made my pain and suffering a mere footnote in my life.

My point to all those who have lost an ability that was dear to them, is to accept it if the loss is permanent. Open your heart and mind to what is. Trust God that good can come from bad. Change is a given in life; some of us are handed a bigger and more challenging share of it. This includes losing abilities as we age. I know now that we can consider these losses as opportunities for doing new things, or maybe old things in a new way. Integrate your changed abilities into the new you. Find meaningful ways to use the abilities you have. My 97-year-old friend Helen uses a walker, but she knits caps, blankets, and mittens for homeless children. What is meaningful is different for everyone. But volunteers are needed to help address a myriad of important societal needs. Take time to be thankful for your blessings. Exercise one way or another. There are classes for all levels of physical ability. Make a new friend; attend a new class; read a new book. If you need help or are just plain lonely, talk to a relative, a minister, a friend. Look around you at the natural beauty of this earth. Make yourself available to listen to someone who needs a friend.

Try talking to God; ask Him to lift your worries and be present in your life.

My message is simple. Every one of us is special and has something special to offer to someone. It does not matter if you have one arm, use a walker, are hearing impaired, or have other physical limitations; you can make a difference to someone. It may mean changing in some way, but I can tell you first hand: change can be wonderful even when it involves a lot of pain and suffering along the way.

Life is precious – take it from someone who came all too close to losing it. Celebrate it every day. "You never know what tomorrow will bring."

13

Study Guide

Chapter 1: The Day

1. The author explains why her work with child safety
   seats was important to her. One of the main problems
   with child safety seats has been incorrect installation,
   which negates the seats' effectiveness in a crash. 96
   percent of parents believe their child safety seats are
   installed properly, but that turns out not to be the
   case. Nationally, at least 70 percent of child safety
   seats are misused (in Oregon we report 80% misuse).
   Consequently, children are put at risk of unnecessary
   injury. The National Highway Traffic Safety Agency
   reports that child safety seats reduce fatal injury by 71
   percent for infants (younger than one year old) and
   by 54 percent for toddlers (one to four years old).

   Did you know that child safety seats are often not
   installed correctly?

Did you know that children should be in a booster seat after they grow out of their child safety seats until they are at least eight years old or four feet nine inches tall? Oregon has passed a law making that a legal requirement.

It is critical that parents and grandparents use child safety seats and use them correctly. If you are in doubt whether you have the correct seat for your child or whether it is installed correctly, go to www. nhtsa.dot.gov. You can find a local child safety seat inspection station, check on the latest child safety seat ease of use ratings, and get the latest data on all aspects of traffic safety. You can also go to www.seatcheck.org or call 1-866-SEATCHECK.

2. The author touches on two ironies surrounding her crash: she was a traffic safety expert and she was near the area where she grew up when the crash occurred. What ironies have you experienced in your life? Did you think that these ironies were remarkable or significant at the time?

3. If you have been in a car crash, were your experiences with pain similar to the author's or very different?

4. If you have been in a car crash, were your experiences with emergency personnel similar or very different?

5. If you have been in a car crash, were your experiences with strangers similar or very different?

6. If you have received a phone call like the author's husband telling you that your loved one had been in a terrible crash and you needed to be at the hospital now, how did you feel?

7. If the author had had breakfast with the police officers the morning of her crash, it seems she would have avoided her life-changing crash. Have you ever not done something that then either helped you avoid a problem or led you into a problem?

8. Do you believe in fate? Why or why not?

9. Is there anything the author should have learned from the crash at this point?

❦

Chapter 2: The Hospital

1. What impression do you get of the teaching hospital the author was in? Would you have felt good about being there?

2. Is the author a cooperative patient? Why? Why not?

3. Does anything upset you about the author's hospital experience?

4. Have you ever had to learn to use a walker? How did you feel when you went out in public with the walker?

5. The author looks to her experiences growing up to explain her reaction to her crash. What childhood or growing-up experiences have shaped your outlook on life?

6. If you have been in a hospital, was your experience similar to the author's or different?

7. When have you or your church prayed for someone who was in the hospital? What was the result of your prayers? How did the result affect you or others who were praying?

8. If you have been in the hospital, when you were allowed to go home, were you prepared? Why? Why not?

⌾⌾⌾

Chapter 3: Marooned in the Family Room

1. Would you agree that the following list of questions would have made the transition to home less difficult?

- What should I expect as far as pain is concerned?

- If I have questions about pain or other concerns, whom do I call? The author had multiple doctors.

- Who will refill my prescriptions? You may have to return to the hospital, as the author's husband had to, to get a narcotic prescription refilled.

- With whom will I have a follow-up appointment and when?

- How can I get transportation for my follow-up appointments?

- What kind of special equipment or furniture do I need at home? Where can I get it?

- What types of things (pain, diarrhea, constipation, bleeding) should I be concerned about?

- How can I wash my hair?

- Do I have any diet restrictions?

2. If you needed a hospital bed or a walker, do you know where you would get one?

3. Would you add any questions to the list above?

4. Would you have insisted on staying longer in the hospital? Why? Why not?

5. How do the author's accommodations sound to you? Do you think her surroundings helped her recovery?

6. Were you surprised about the author's lack of negative feelings about the woman driver who hit her? How would you have felt?

7. Did you find any humor in the author's situation or experiences?

8. What did you learn about the author's personality during this chapter?

❧❧❧

Chapter 4: Meet the Family Caregivers

1. Were you surprised about how reluctant the author was to leave her home "for fun"?

2. Were you surprised how the author was treated by clerks when she was in a wheelchair? If you have a disability, have your experiences been similar or different?

3. Do you think "mothers are their daughters' compass"?

4. How would you describe the relationship the author and her husband have?

5. If you were suddenly placed in a situation where you had to be the caregiver for a loved one, do you think you would be willing to do it?

6. What relationships do you value?

Chapter 5: Rehabilitation

1. Were you surprised about the location of the physical therapy facility?

2. If you have been to a physical therapy facility, how was it similar or different?

3. If you have needed physical therapy in the past, what helped or did not help with your problem?

4. Were you surprised that the author considered not having the surgery on her ankle and foot? Why? Why not?

5. How do you make difficult decisions?

6. How would you describe the author's interest in getting back to work? Do you think it helped her

recovery? Do you think your attitude would be similar or different?

7. How would you feel if your spouse bought a new car on her or his own?

8. Why do you think the author made the car purchase decision so quickly and on her own? Do you think you would do the same thing?

⌘

Chapter 6: Trying to Work Things Out

1. Is your attitude toward work similar to the author's?

2. The author thinks her childhood had a great deal to do with her attitude toward work. Did your childhood have anything to do with shaping your attitude toward work?

3. Which of the author's traits do you think really helped in her recovery? Which did not help? Do you have similar traits that have helped or not helped you in a difficult time?

4. The author seems to think very positively about her childhood even though it was filled with hard work. Why? What was positive about your childhood?

5. The author chose to close down her consulting business and go to work part-time for the traffic safety nonprofit she had started. Do you think that was a good decision?

6. Do you have uninsured/underinsured auto insurance? Does the author convince you about its importance?

7. The author describes having a difficult time with lawyers regarding her umbrella insurance. Have you had similar feelings regarding lawyers or the legal system?

8. Why do you think the insurance problems created tension between the author and her husband?

9. Why do you think the author eventually stopped working altogether? Do you think that was a good decision?

10. Have you ever had to give up on something you really enjoyed? How did you feel?

❧◦❧

Chapter 7: New Directions

1. Were you surprised when the author chose to volunteer so soon after leaving work? Why do you think the author chose to volunteer?

2. Do you think it was a good idea that the author volunteered?

3. Did volunteering help or hurt her return to good health?

4. What has been your experience with volunteering?

5. The author feels that it is critically important to have disability insurance. The Insurance Information Institute reports that 43 percent of all people now age 40 will suffer some long-term disability by age 65. According to the U.S. Census Bureau, individuals have a one in five chance of becoming disabled.

Do you have disability insurance? If you do, does it require you to work at any job, not just the one you have as a profession?

6. The author and her husband argued over pursuing the disability insurance benefits but found a way to resolve the issue that was acceptable to both of them. Have you and your spouse or partner handled disagreements in a similar fashion? What does it take to resolve differences?

7. What do you think about the way in which the author pursued receiving disability insurance benefits? Do you agree she should have pursued it?

8. What changes did you notice in the author as a result of her volunteering experiences?

9. Why did the author take so long to truly change? Have you ever had to undergo serious change?

⊱◈⊰

Chapter 8: Knowing and Doing What Matters: Faith

1. Do you agree that the author's life was out of balance before her crash? Why? Why not?

2. Do you agree with the author that children can help you keep a balance in your life? What if you do not have children?

3. Have you defined what "milk" is for you? Have you figured out a plan of action that is consistent with your goals?

4. Do you think God was punishing the author?

5. Who helps you with your concerns and problems? Have you found prayer helpful?

6. Does your definition of church differ from the author's?

7. Have you ever experienced God's presence?

8. Do you set aside time for reflection or meditation? If yes, how does it help you?

9. Why didn't this near fatal crash ruin the author's life?

10. Do you think God has a detailed plan for each of our lives?

11. If you have had to deal with a personal crisis or life-changing event, did your relationship with God strengthen, or did you pull away from or blame God?

12. Has any good come out of this crash?

13. Is nature as special to you as it has become to the author? What have you observed today?

14. Do you have a plan for your life? How does it fit with the Jeremiah scripture quoted by the author?

⌒∂⌒

Chapter 9: Knowing and Doing What Matters: Family and Friends

1. How do you think the author felt about needing to rely on family and friends for all her daily activities? How do you think you would feel?

2. Has your family needed to respond to a family member's crisis? What did you learn?

3. Do you think friends are important to your well-being? Why? Do you think you have enough friends? Do you spend time with your friends?

4. What does it mean to you to "seek first to understand"? What has been your experience in trying to understand other people's positions?

5. Have you been able to ask for or accept help when you have needed it?

6. Were you surprised that the author did not feel lucky for a while after the crash? After all, she could have died.

7. The author discusses having to give up several activities she had always loved to do. Have you had to forego things you had enjoyed due to a change in your health? Was it hard for you to give these activities up? What or who helped you accept the changes?

8. Can you name a few of your blessings – good things that have happened to you?

Chapter 10: Knowing and Doing What Matters: Health (Physical and Mental)

1. Do you agree with the author that exercise is important?

2. Do you exercise? How often? Does it help you?

3. Do you think one needs to enjoy exercising in order to do it? Why or why not?

4. The author mentions studies that show people heal faster when therapy includes gardening. Why do you think gardening helps healing?

5. Do you make time in your life for learning? What are your interests?

6. Is there something you look forward to learning to do in the future?

7. The author enjoys listening to educational or news programs on the radio. Do you ever choose to listen to the radio with the objective of learning?

8. The author thinks that learning is important for mental health. Would you agree?

Chapter 11: Knowing and Doing What Matters: Helping Others

1. The author makes the point that she has always had helping others as a priority. The type of help she provided changed throughout her life. Has your experience been similar or different?

2. Do you find her points about volunteering convincing? Do you think volunteering is only for retirees?

3. Where and when have you volunteered? Was it a good experience?

4. Is helping others a priority in your life? Why? Why not?

5. Are you able to say "no" to requests for doing things you do not want to do?

6. The author uses a chart to take a look at all of her priorities to see if she has a balanced life. Do you think the author has a balanced life now? Why? Why not?

7. Make a chart of your activities and see if you think your life is balanced. Are the headings in the chart different? Even if your headings are different, do your activities still include time spent in the areas

of: Helping Others, Family/Friends, Health, and Faith? Why or why not?

8. On what parts of your life do you place the most value?

9. Do you think a person who is working a 40-hour work week can have a balanced life? Why? Why not?

ᴄᴏᴏᴄᴏ

Chapter 12: Decide to Change

1. Does the author make a good case for accepting permanent loss and choosing to make the best of it?

2. Do you really think everyone can help someone if they choose to?

3. The author has talked about a variety of changes she had to make. Have you experienced a loss in physical or mental ability? Have you been able to make changes and move on in a way that brings joy and peace?

4. Do you think the author's life is actually better now than before C-Day? If yes, better in what ways?

5. What is the message you take away from the author's memoir?

6. Has this book motivated you to make any changes in your life?

LaVergne, TN USA
15 May 2010
182823LV00002B/1/P